OLD ROSES

DAVID AUSTIN

GARDEN·ART·PRESS

ISBN: 978 1 87067 369 3

(Parts of this text originally appeared in *Old Roses & English Roses* by David Austin, 1993
and *The Rose* by David Austin, 2009)

British Library Cataloguing-in-Publication Data:
A catalogue record for this book is available from the British Library

Front Cover: R x centifolia *Muscosa* (see p.86)
Back Cover: Top Left: Souvenir du Docteur Jamain (see p.171);
Top Right: Hebe's Lip (see p.52); Bottom Left: Félicité Parmentier (see p.68);
Bottom Right: Violacea (see p.46)
Front Endpaper: *Mutabilis* (see p.108).
Back Endpaper: Comte de Chambord (see p.116)
Frontispiece: Madame Isaac Pereire (see p.134)
Title Page: Duchesse d'Angoulême (see p.31)

Printed in China for Garden Art Press, an imprint of the Antique Collectors' Club Ltd.,
Woodbridge, Suffolk IP12 4SD

CONTENTS

INTRODUCTION

Garden roses fall into two very different groups which are usually described as the Old Roses and the Modern Roses. Most of the Old Roses were introduced before 1900, while most of the Modern Roses were introduced afterwards. There is, however, a great deal of overlap on both sides of that date. The Old Roses have flowers of quite a different style to those of the Modern Roses (by which I mean the Hybrid Teas and Floribundas of today). The beauty of the Old Rose lies in the open flower and a more natural shrubby habit of growth, while the Modern Roses are bedding roses of short, upright habit whose beauty usually lies in the unfolding bud.

The Old Garden Roses have been with us for centuries, starting almost at the dawn of civilisation in the Middle East – spreading first to Greece and later to Rome and thence to Europe as a whole. They are distinguished by their open flowers, usually in the form of a rosette but often cupped shape and sometimes of a more domed shape with recurving petals. Such flowers may have many petals or few; they may be loosely built or closely packed with petals, resulting in a great variety of shapes. They may also be double or semi-double. Above all, the majority of them are very fragrant.

The Old Roses began to lose their popularity in the latter part of the 19th century and by the early part of the 20th century had almost disappeared from our gardens in the face of competition from the all-conquering Hybrid Teas. Fortunately for us, no sooner had they almost vanished when certain collectors started to preserve them in their own gardens. Writing in the Royal Horticultural Society's Journal in 1896, George Paul exclaimed: 'Wanted: a refuge for the Old Roses where they may be found again when tastes change.' He was, in fact, showing remarkable insight, for within little more than a quarter of a century such outstanding gardeners as Edward Bunyard, G.N. Smith, George Beckwith, Maud Messel, Constance Spry, Ruby Fleischmann, Murray Hornibrook, A.T. Johnson, Bobbie James, Anastasia Law and Vita Sackville-West were already gathering together collections of Old Roses.

It is, however, to Graham Thomas that we owe the greatest debt. It was he who put together all these collections into one great collection – and, indeed, added many more as Nursery Manager first at Hillings & Co. of Woking and later at Sunningdale Nurseries. His collection of different varieties numbered well into four figures and from these nurseries the old varieties spread into many gardens in the UK and eventually into nurseries around the world, so that we now have a movement which is continually gathering momentum.

In this book I cover all the most worthwhile of the Old Roses. In a companion volume in the series I extend this to their natural successors, The English Roses, which I began breeding in the 1940s to combine the fragrance and beauty of Old Roses with the repeat-flowering abilities and wider colour range of Modern Roses. The third book in the series looks at Climbing Roses, and the fourth considers Modern Bush and Shrub Roses.

Dating back to the 16th century or earlier, **Rosa gallica** *Versicolor (Rosa Mundi) flowers in profusion, providing a wonderful massed effect*

THE OLD ROSES

Throughout the course of history, from the very earliest times to the present day, the rose has been the single flower closest to Man's heart. Over the centuries it has proved itself an enduring favourite among gardeners in the western world and more recently its popularity has spread far and wide to other, more distant parts of our planet. Fortunately it has a great adaptability and will grow and thrive in a variety of climates. In fact so strongly favoured is the rose that it is now planted and found valiantly struggling to survive in even the most unsuitable of habitats.

Why the rose should be so widely admired is easier to explain visually than it is to put into words, but one certainty is that it is very different in character to other plants. The best explanation I can give is that, to me at least, the rose

has a certain charm and humanity that we do not find in any other flower. There is also an informality about the flower that is unique and growth tends to be rampant and almost out of control – though not quite. Both these are qualities that we might describe as being very human. This would explain why the rose, over its long history, has always been used as a symbol of love and beauty.

In Greek mythology, Aphrodite, goddess of love, was regarded as the creator of the rose. She is said to have been pricked by the thorns of a rosebush while attempting to help her mortally wounded lover Adonis, with a mix of her blood and their tears bringing forth the red rose. Similarly, in Roman legend the rose was held to have sprung from the blood of the Roman goddess of love, Venus. Again and again, throughout ancient history, the rose crops up as a symbol of love and beauty – and sometimes even of licentiousness and excess.

With the rise of Christianity, the rose was at first looked upon with disapproval because of its pagan past, but this attitude soon changed and before long we find the rose becoming intertwined with the Christian faith: for example, the rosary and the idea of the five petals of the rose representing the five wounds of Christ. The red rose was eventually adopted as a symbol of the blood of Christian martyrs, while roses also later came to be associated with the Virgin Mary. Indeed, it was the Church which was to a large degree responsible for carrying the rose across Europe to many other lands.

But although we in the West, and in Britain in particular, like to think of the rose as being very much our own, this is by no means entirely true. Roses appear at one time or another in association with Brahma, Buddha, Mahomet, Vishnu and Confucius, and the origins of the roses we enjoy today lie to a large degree in the lands of the Middle and Far East. This is perhaps best summed up in the following extract from Vita Sackville-West's long poem The Garden (1946):

> 'June of the iris and the rose,
> The rose not English as we fondly think,
> Anacreon and Bion sang the rose;
> And Rhodes the isle whose very name means rose
> Struck roses on her coins;
> Pliny made lists and Roman libertines
> Made wreaths to war among the flutes and wines;
> The young Crusaders found the Syrian rose
> Springing from Saracenic quoins,
> And China opened her shut gate
> To let her roses through, and Persian shrines
> Of poetry and painting gave the rose.'

This exquisite miniature painting on silk by an unknown artist from around 1450 shows the Persian Prince Humay meeting the Chinese Princess Humayan in a rose garden

It's true to say that it is in poetry and literature that affection for the rose is most vividly proclaimed, both for the beauty of the rose itself and as a

symbol of all that is best and most beautiful in human nature. As early as the 5th century BC, the Greek lyric poet Anacreon penned what is probably the first poem to the rose :

> I sing of Spring, flower crowned
> I sing the praises of the Rose
> Friend aid me in my song.
> The Rose is the perfume of the Gods,
> > the joy of men,
> It adorns the Graces at the blossoming
> > of Love,
> It is the favoured flower of Venus,
> It is the chief care of the Nymphs,
> It is the joy of the Muses,
> In spite of its many thorns
> We gather it with delight.

The Bible mentions the rose on numerous occasions and of course Shakespeare, in his plays and sonnets, alludes to the rose more than 60 times – as for instance when Juliet, exasperated by the damaging hatred between her own Capulet family and her lover Romeo's Montague clan, asks:

> 'What's in a name? That which we call a rose
> By any other name would smell as sweet.'

Scottish poet Robbie Burns proclaimed in 1794:

> 'O, my luve's like a red, red rose,
> That's newly sprung in June'

and nearly a century later, John Keats enthused in his sonnet To a Friend who Sent Me some Roses:

> 'But when, O Wells! thy roses came to me
> My sense with their deliciousness was
> > spell'd:
> Soft voices had they, that with tender plea
> Whisper'd of peace and truth, and
> > friendliness unquell'd.'

'Roses' from the Nassau Florilegium *by 17th-century botanical artist Johann Walther of Strasbourg, a volume of paintings commissioned by the Court of Nassau to celebrate the garden of rare plants and flowers at his castle at Idstein, near Frankfurt*

The rose also has a long and distinguished history in art, and the earliest known representation of a rose was found at the palace of Knossos, on the Greek island of Crete, in a delicate fresco thought to date from between 1700 and 2000 BC. From the Renaissance onwards it was painted frequently, often for its own sake, and this was particularly so in the paintings of the Dutch school of the late 16th and 17th centuries, including works by Jan Brueghel, Jan Davidsz de Heem and Daniel Seghers. The French painter Henri Fantin-Latour (1836-1904) was also well-known for his paintings of flowers, especially roses.

As decoration, too, the rose stands supreme above all other flowers and has featured on pottery and fabrics, in sculpture and as a decoration of all kinds in all ages across many lands. Indeed it is unusual to walk into any house in the West without finding some sort of representation of a rose. This, I think, illustrates better than anything else the very special place the rose holds in our lives. I remember talking to the chief designer from one of our largest firms of pottery manufacturers who told me that the rose is by far the most popular decoration for china and pottery, the demand for rose designs exceeding those of all other flowers put together.

In the flower of a rose there are many flowers. It is seldom quite the same on any two days. From the opening of the bud to the fall of the flower, at every turn of its petals as they unfold, it is always presenting us with a different picture. Its colouring, too, is the same: perhaps deep and rich at the centre, maybe softer towards the outer edges, but the balance will always be changing, sometimes paling with time or taking on a new hue, or occasionally intensifying. The flower varies according to where it is grown, from garden to garden, from one soil to another. It varies according to weather conditions too; it will be quite different on a sunny day than on one which is cool and overhung. It will take on one appearance in early summer and quite another in the autumn. Here perhaps is one reason we do not easily tire of it.

Between one variety and another, from one class to another, and from species to species, the rose has many forms. The flower may, for example, be in the form of a rosette as in the old Alba Rose 'Queen of Denmark'; it may be a rounded cup as in the Bourbon Rose 'Reine Victoria'. Then there are the heavy, voluptuous blooms of Rosa centifolia and the wide open semi-double flowers of Damask 'Celsiana' with its long stamens.

However, the rose appeals to us not only for its visual appearance but for its wonderful fragrance or, should I say, fragrances – for these take on many beautiful shades. Among roses we can find nearly all the fragrances to be found in flowers, making it no surprise that the rose fragrance is the basis for most manufactured perfumes. Old roses are particularly fragrant, encapsulated by the heady aromas of the Centifolias and Damasks, and such a wonderful quality is this that it has been one of the things I have been most anxious to preserve and enhance in the development of my English Roses. The sense of smell is a hard one to tie down; it is the least developed of our senses, yet it has great power to move us.

Man has taken a wild flower and over many centuries, at first by the selection of chance seedlings and later by design, moulded it to his wishes. Today roses are to be found in almost every country in the world; so what is the fascination of this flower? How is it that the rose has always been the best loved of all flowers? It seems to have the ability to evoke by its beauty (and, to some degree, the long accumulation of its history) many of the emotions, principles, desires and joys fundamental to the spirit of man. For this reason, it is worthy of closer attention than we would afford other flowers; for the rose is more than other flowers – it is part of the very fabric of our lives; it has about it a humanity that we do not find in any other garden plant.

An excellent garden shrub which develops into an arching mound of growth, **Cardinal de Richelieu** *is one of the darkest of all roses and makes a strong impact in any setting*

Part 1

THE ORIGINAL OLD ROSES

Included in this section are those classes which were established prior to the introduction of the repeat-flowering China Rose at the end of the eighteenth century, that is to say the Gallicas, the Damasks, the Albas, the Centifolias and the Moss Roses. As most readers will be aware, these are not small upright bushes, as are Modern Hybrid Teas, but genuine shrubs like any other shrub in the garden. Their growth will reach somewhere in the region of 90cm–1.8m / 3–6ft. according to variety, although there are among them many shorter shrubs that fit nicely into a small garden.

The formation of the flowers of the Old Roses is quite different to that to which we have become accustomed today. In the Modern Rose the ideal lies in the bud with its high-pointed centre, and this is indeed often beautiful, but the disadvantage is that the mature flower tends to be muddled and almost completely lacking in form. Old Roses are quite different; their buds, though often charming, are likely to open as small cups, with little petals developing within, but it is as the flower gradually expands into the full bloom that its true beauty is revealed. At this later stage it can take on many forms: it may remain cupped, it may become flat with many petals, or it may reflex at the edges to form an almost domed flower. Between these shapes there are many gradations. The flower may also, of course, be semi-double, exposing an airy bunch of stamens at the centre. Thus we have a bloom that is beautiful at all stages, from the opening of the bud to the eventual fall of the petals. It is this variety of form that makes these roses so worthwhile. Fine as the Hybrid Tea may be, the Old Roses offer so much more scope, and for this reason we have, at our nursery, thought it worthwhile to proceed further with the breeding of roses of the old type.

It has to be admitted that Old Roses are rather limited in their colour range. We have white through pink all the way to a maroon-crimson, mauve and purple —all colours often of exceptional purity and softness of tone. Susan Williams-Ellis (who spent many weeks at our nursery painting roses for her Portmeirion Pottery) speaking in terms of fabrics has suggested that these are like vegetable dyes in comparison with the harsher 'chemical' colours of Modern Roses. I think this puts it rather well. There are, unfortunately, only one or two yellows and not many whites, although 'Madame Hardy' and 'Madame Legras de Saint Germain' can produce some of the most perfect blooms. Pink is the true colour

Facing page, **R. gallica officinalis***, a rose of great antiquity, known as the Apothecary's Rose because it was grown for its medicinal qualities as well as for perfume and preserves*

of the rose, and in the Old Roses it often has a clarity rarely found elsewhere. The colour crimson is seldom pure in these early roses, but it does have the great virtue of turning to wonderful shades of purple, violet and mauve.

The Old Roses of this section do have one disadvantage, if in fact it can be truly described as a disadvantage; they flower only once in a season, whereas their successors are repeat flowering. It should, however, be borne in mind that we expect no more of any other shrub. We do not, for example, expect repeat flowering of the lilac or the rhododendron. If your garden is reasonably large, you may not wish to have all your roses in flower throughout the summer, even though you will probably like to have at least some in bloom later in the season. You may prefer that they should take their place in due season, like any other flower. It should also be remembered that a rose which flowers but once tends to give a better show for that limited period, during which it is able to devote all its energy to one glorious burst of flowers. It will also usually form a more shapely shrub for, unlike bush roses, shrub roses produce long growth from the base of the plant. This does not flower in the first season but subsequently sends out flowering branches. It is this strong growth that forms the basic structure of a well-shaped shrub which is not only more pleasing to the eye, but which also displays its flowers in a more natural and satisfactory manner.

Almost all these roses are over one hundred years old, and one or two may well be over a thousand years old. There must have been many more of their brethren who have fallen by the wayside. Those that remain really are great survivors. It is, therefore, not surprising that they are extremely tough and hardy. It is our experience that they are also more disease resistant than most Hybrid Teas and Floribundas, mildew being their worst fault, though this is not difficult to control. They are easy to grow and will do well with minimal care, although a little extra attention can yield rich rewards.

The rose has received far more attention from the plant breeder than any other flower, so it may seem strange that so many gardeners should turn back to the beginning and start growing varieties from the distant past. There is little doubt this has something to do with the attractions of the antique, and I see no reason to decry this. There is, however, much more to the Old Roses than this, for they possess a very special charm that is not always to be found in roses of more recent date.

It is my personal opinion that we are today much too obsessed with the past, and often too little concerned with the creations of our own time. If we consider the devotion that we put into the preservation of old buildings and how little concern we show for new ones, it sometimes seems a little unhealthy. Having said this, there is a certain satisfaction to be gained from the sheer permanence of the Old Roses; we have had time to get to know them and to love them, something that cannot be said for Modern Roses that come and go with bewildering speed. In spite of this, it cannot be stressed too strongly that Old Roses are not mere curiosities but first-class shrubs in their own right, and their gentle colours and more natural growth melt perfectly into the garden scheme. Finally, but by no means least, it is hardly necessary to say that, with the exception of the English Roses, their fragrance excels that of the majority of those which have come after them.

The naming of Old Roses is always a source of controversy and many Old Rose enthusiasts like to show their knowledge on the subject. These roses suffered a long period of neglect before re-emerging in our time, and inevitably many names were lost. Although a great deal of research has gone into finding the correct names, this has not always been possible. A description we find in an old book or catalogue may have been adequate for the gardeners of that time, but is frequently insufficient for us to give a name to a particular rose. It has often been necessary simply to do the best that we can, and, in fact, this does not matter very much, for as we all know, a rose by any other name would smell as sweet. The important thing is to agree on a name so that we all know what we are talking about.

Now that we have the English Roses, the question arises, 'Do we any longer need the Old Roses?' English Roses are hybrids between the Old Roses and the Modern. They have much of the particular kind of beauty of an Old Rose and similar shrubby growth, and yet are regularly repeat flowering and have a much wider range of colour. I, for one, would not like to be without the Old Roses or, indeed, any others. The rose changes in mood over the generations. We never quite regain that particular kind of beauty that belongs to roses of another age. The beauty of a rose is not something that can ever be repeated, any more than an artist can ever repeat a picture from the past.

Madame Legras de Saint Germain
is a rose of exceptional beauty with a strong and delicious fragrance

Gallica Roses

Rosa gallica is a native of central and southern Europe. It forms an upright shrub of 1m / 3ft in height which suckers freely, with slender stems and many small thorns. It bears deep pink flowers of 5–7cm / 2–3in across, followed by round, red hips. Our garden Gallicas of today have been developed over the centuries from this species.

Although so much of the history of Old Roses is shrouded in mystery, it is safe to assume that the Gallicas are the oldest of garden roses and have been involved, to a greater or lesser extent, in the development of all the four other classes of Old Roses. Their influence is present, at least in some small degree, in nearly all our garden roses of today. Long before they received their name, their predecessors were grown by both the Greeks and Romans and almost certainly by others before them. Although they are the oldest of the truly Old Roses, they also became the most highly developed. In 1629, the great English botanist and gardener John Parkinson listed twelve varieties. A little later the Dutch began raising seedlings to produce new varieties. It was not long before the French started breeding them on a large scale and they became known as Gallicas. Soon after 1800 there were said to be over one thousand varieties. Most of these have long since been lost, but we still have more of them than any other group of the truly 'old' roses, and these include some of the most beautiful roses that can be grown today.

Not surprisingly, all this work led to highly developed flowers in a variety of colours. These tend to be in the stronger shades: deep pinks and near crimsons, as well as rich mixtures of purple, violet and mauve. There are a number of good striped varieties as well as others that are attractively mottled, marbled or flecked, and there are also a few soft pinks, though these are probably hybrids of other classes. No other Old Rose produces such subtle and fascinating mixtures of colour. They are nearly all very fragrant.

The Gallica Rose or, as it is sometimes called, the 'Rose of Provins', is not difficult to recognise. It usually forms a small shrub, generally not more than 1.2m / 4ft in height, with strong, rather upright growth and numerous small, bristly thorns. The leaves are oval, pointed at the tip, of rather rough texture and often dark green in colour. The flowers are usually held either singly or in threes, and the buds are typically of spherical shape.

These roses are excellent garden subjects, with low, easily managed growth that is ideal for the smaller garden. They will, if required, grow in poor, even gravelly soil, and demand a minimum of attention. If grown on their own roots they will sucker freely and quickly spread across a border. Although they are often effective when grown in this manner, they can become a problem and for this reason it is usually better to plant budded stock and not to plant too deeply.

Alain Blanchard This variety has almost single flowers of deep purple-crimson, with contrasting golden stamens, the colour later turning to a purple which is attractively dotted and mottled with pink. Its growth is thorny, about 1.2m / 4ft in height, with pale green foliage. Fragrant. Probably a Gallica / Centifolia cross. Bred by Vibert (France), introduced 1839.

*Cupped in shape, the nearly single flowers of **Alain Blanchard** are crimson at first with a boss of golden stamens*

*The perfectly flat flowers of **Anaïs Ségalas** fade from mauve-crimson to pale lilac-pink*

*Facing page, **Beau Narcisse** is a beautiful, and in many ways typical Gallica, whose crimson flowers are speckled with purple*

Anaïs Ségalas This rose has perfectly shaped flowers which open flat and are well filled with petals, showing a green eye at the centre. The colour is a rich mauve-crimson, turning with age to a pale lilac-pink. It forms a low-growing, branching and free-flowering bush with light green foliage. Strong fragrance. Height 1m / 3ft. Bred by Vibert (France), introduced 1837.

Assemblages des Beautés ('Rouge Éblouissante') Very double flowers of a vivid cherry-red, unusual amongst Gallicas; later becoming tinged with mauve, the petals reflexing almost to a ball, with a button eye at the centre. Very fragrant. Height 1.2m / 4ft. Introduced by Delaage in 1823.

Beau Narcisse A rather short and unassuming rose but beautiful in detail. The flowers are medium sized, no more than about 5cm / 2in across and crimson, speckled with purple, the reverse of the petals being paler. It has bushy, quite wiry growth about 1.2m / 4ft. tall. There is a good fragrance. Bred by Miellez (France) before 1828.

Belle de Crécy One of the finest, most free-flowering and reliable of Gallica Roses. On opening the flowers are a cerise-pink mixed with mauve, later turning to soft Parma-violet and ultimately to lavender-grey; a wonderful succession of tints. They are shapely in form, the petals opening wide and reflexing to expose a button centre. A very rich fragrance. This variety will grow to about 1.2m / 4ft in height and about 1m / 3ft across. Bred by Roeser prior to 1848.

Belle Isis A charming little rose of short growth that is ideal for the small garden. The flowers are not large but are full petalled, opening flat, neatly formed and of a delicate flesh-pink colour. It has tough, sturdy growth, with many prickles and small light green leaves. Its origins are something of a mystery as it is unusual to find so delicate a pink among the Gallicas, but it is probable that one of its parents was a Centifolia. It has the unusual fragrance of myrrh, and this would seem to indicate there is also Ayrshire 'Splendens' in its make up, for this scent was unique to those roses. Height 1m / 3ft. Bred by Parmentier (Belgium), introduced 1845.

Belle de Crécy is one of the most free-flowering and reliable of Gallica Roses, with petals that open wide to reveal a button centre

*Facing page, The origin of **Belle Isis** is something of a mystery as it is unusual to find so delicate a pink, a myrrh fragrance and such a short, neat shrub amongst the Gallicas*

Burgundiaca is a truly miniature Gallica with distinct close-jointed growth bearing one-inch flowers

Burgundiaca (Burgundy Rose, 'Parviflora', 'Pompon de Bourgogne') A charming miniature Gallica which forms a dense, very short-jointed shrub, with very small dark green pointed leaves and tiny claret-coloured pompon flowers made up of numerous small petals. It is as though a large shrub had shrunk in all its parts, resulting in something quite unlike any other rose. The growth is about 1m / 3ft in height. It can become rather too narrowly upright, but careful clipping will enable it to maintain its shape. In existence before 1664.

Camaieux One of the most pleasing of the striped roses. Its flowers are only loosely double but of shapely formation. They are white and heavily striped and splashed with a crimson that soon turns to purple, later becoming pale lilac and remaining attractive at all stages. There is a sweet and spicy fragrance. It forms a small shrub of about 1m / 3ft in height. Introduced by Gendron in 1826.

Camaieux
bears striped flowers that are loosely double but of shapely formation

Charles de Mills *is among the largest-flowered and most spectacular of the Old Roses*

Facing page, ***Cardinal de Richelieu*** *is one of the darkest of all roses. The flowers are mauvish-pink in the bud, becoming mauve, and ending in the richest purple*

Cardinal de Richelieu One of the darkest of all roses. The flowers are mauvish-pink in the bud, becoming mauve, and ending in the richest pure purple. They are quite small and as they develop the petals reflex back almost forming a ball. This is an excellent garden shrub, developing into an arching mound of growth with dark green leaves and few thorns. It requires good cultivation and fairly severe pruning if it is to attain its full potential, otherwise the flowers may be rather insignificant. It is advisable to thin out the shrub by the annual removal of some of its older growth. The height is 1.5m / 5ft. Fragrant. Bred by Parmentier prior to 1847.

Charles de Mills The largest flowered and most spectacular of the Old Roses. Each bloom has numerous evenly placed petals which open so flat that they give the impression of having been sliced off with a sharp knife. The colour is rich purple-crimson, gradually turning to pure purple. It is an erect grower but forms a rather floppy shrub of 1.2m / 4ft in height and may require some support. Unfortunately there is no more than a slight fragrance. Introduced about 1790.

Cramoisi Picotée A pretty and unusual little rose with small, full, almost pompon flowers which are crimson in the bud, opening to a deep pink with crimson at the edges. The growth is short and compact with small dark green leaves. There is little fragrance. Height 1m / 3ft. Bred by Vibert (France), introduced 1834.

D'Aguesseau This rose has the brightest red colouring to be found among the Gallicas. For this reason we find it is in great demand—perhaps greater demand than its qualities warrant. Its colour is a bright cerise-scarlet although this soon fades to cerise-pink. The flowers are full petalled and fragrant, the growth strong with ample foliage. Height 1.5m / 5ft. Bred by Vibert (France), introduced 1837.

Duc de Guiche A magnificent Gallica with large flowers of a rich wine-crimson shaded with purple. They have many petals and are beautifully formed, opening at first to a cup and gradually reflexing. It is one of the finest of its class, but in a dry season the colour can become dull and altogether less pleasing, particularly in light soils. Height about 1.2m / 4ft. Fragrant. Bred by Prévost, introduced 1829.

*Full-petalled and fragrant, **D'Aguesseau** has the brightest red colouring to be found among the Gallicas*

Duchesse d'Angoulême This little charmer is probably not wholly Gallica. The delicacy of its transparent, blush-pink, globular flowers, which hang so gracefully from its arching growth, strongly suggests some other influence — *Rosa centifolia* has been suggested, but it is difficult to be sure. It has few thorns, light green foliage and a spreading growth to about 1m / 3ft in height and as much across. It was, at one time, also known as the 'Wax Rose'. Bred by Vibert (France), prior to 1821.

Duchesse de Buccleugh A variety with unusually large flowers that open flat and quartered with a button eye. Their colour is an intense magenta-pink which does not appeal to everyone. The growth is very strong and upright, to 1.8m / 6ft in height, with fine luxurious foliage. One of the latest of the Gallicas to flower. Bred by Vibert (France), introduced 1837.

*Once known as the 'Wax Rose', **Duchesse d'Angoulême** has blush-pink globular flowers hanging gracefully from arching growth and is probably not wholly Gallica*

Duchesse de Montebello A rather loose-growing shrub bearing sprays of soft pink, full-petalled flowers of open-cupped formation. These have a delicate charm and blend nicely with its grey-green foliage. It is unlikely that it is a true Gallica. I have used it for breeding purposes crossing it with repeat-flowering English Roses and, much to my surprise, obtained a proportion of repeat-flowering seedlings. This would suggest that it was itself the result of a cross with a repeat-flowering rose. Such mysteries contribute much to the interest of Old Roses. A beautiful rose with a sweet fragrance. Height 1.2m / 4ft. Bred by Laffay (France), introduced prior to 1829.

Du Maître d'École ('De La Maître d'École') A variety producing some of the largest flowers found among Gallicas. They are full-petalled and open flat and quartered, later reflexing to reveal a button centre. Their colour is a deep pink, gradually turning to lilac-pink and taking on mauve and coppery shading as the flowers age. The growth is lax, about 1–1.2m / 3–4ft in height, arching under the weight of its heavy, fragrant blooms. Coquereau (France) 1831.

*Facing page, **Duchesse de Montebello** bears sprays of soft pink, full-petalled flowers of open-cupped formation*

*The flowers of **Du Maître d'École**, which are some of the largest found among the Gallicas, start out deep pink then turn lilac-pink before taking on mauve and coppery tints as they age*

Empress Josephine (Impératrice Joséphine) An entirely appropriate name for one of the most beautiful Old Roses. Josephine perhaps did more than anyone else to establish and encourage interest in roses throughout Europe, gathering together at Malmaison the largest collection of roses ever established up to her time. This variety is far removed from the typical Gallica and is classed as *Rosa × francofurtana*. It is probably a hybrid of *R. cinnamomea*. The flowers are semi-double with wavy petals of an unusual papery appearance. Their colour is a rich Tyrian rose veined with a deeper shade. Unlike the majority of Old Roses, the flowers are followed by a fine crop of large turbinate hips. 'Empress Josephine' forms a low, shapely, rather flat growing bush some 1m / 3ft in height, with very coarse textured grey-green foliage and few thorns. Excellent in every way, the only possible complaint being that it has no more than a faint fragrance. It has one close relative, 'Agatha', which is of the same class, but which is an altogether taller and coarser rose with, rather surprisingly, an intense fragrance. Bred by Descemet 1815.

Empress Josephine (and facing page) is far removed from the typical Gallica. The flowers are semi-double with wavy petals of an unusual papery appearance and, unlike the majority of Old Roses, they are followed by a fine crop of large red hips

With excellent garden qualities, **R. gallica officinalis** *is the oldest cultivated form of the Gallica Rose and is said to be the 'Red Rose of Lancaster'*

R. gallica officinalis (the Apothecary's Rose) This historic rose is said to be the 'Red Rose of Lancaster', the emblem chosen by the House of Lancaster at the time of the Wars of the Roses, and there is little doubt it is the oldest cultivated form of the Gallica Rose that we have. It seems to have first appeared in Europe in the town of Provins, south east of Paris, where it was used in the making of perfume. It was said to have been brought there by Thibault Le Chansonnier on his return from the Crusades. Thibault IV, King of Navarre, wrote the poem *Le Roman de la Rose* in about 1260, and in it he refers to this rose as the rose from the 'Land of the Saracens'. Whatever the truth may be, this is a rose of great antiquity. For centuries it was grown for its medicinal qualities, and for this reason it is known as the Apothecary's Rose. Today we appreciate it for its excellent garden qualities, for it certainly deserves a place among the very finest of garden shrubs of any kind. It forms low branching growth, carries its semi-double, light crimson, fragrant flowers (with golden stamens) nicely poised above ample dark green foliage, blooms very freely, and provides a most satisfactory effect in the border. If grown on its own roots it will quickly spread by suckering and might well be used on banks and in other areas where ground cover is required. Budded on a stock it will grow to about 1.2m / 4ft in height and about the same across. The colour varies widely according to climate and season and is much paler under hot conditions. In autumn it produces small round hips which are not without ornamental value.

R. gallica Versicolor (Rosa Mundi) This is a striped sport of *R. g* var. *officinalis*, having all the virtues of that excellent rose, to which it is similar in every respect except colour. This is palest blush-pink, clearly striped and splashed with light crimson which provides an attractively fresh appearance. Occasionally a flower will revert to the colour of its parent. It has the same strong bushy growth, and flowers in the same happy profusion, providing a wonderful massed effect. Both roses make fine low hedges—indeed it would be hard to find better roses for this purpose. The date of this rose is not known, but it certainly goes back as far as the sixteenth century and earlier. Like its parent it will make a 1.2 x 1.2m/4 x 4ft shrub.

R. gallica *Versicolor* *has all the virtues of its parent* R. g. var. officinalis, *with the same strong bushy growth, and flowers in profusion*

Gallica Roses

Georges Vibert Rather small flowers which open flat, with narrow quilled petals of blush pink striped with light crimson. The growth is narrow and upright, about 1.5m / 5ft in height, with many thorns and unusually small leaves. Bred by Bizard (France) 1828.

Gloire de France A small shrub with somewhat spreading growth of 1m / 3ft in height and rather more across. It bears beautifully shaped, full lilac-pink flowers with reflexing petals which hold their colour at the centre while paling with age towards the edges. Strongly fragrant. Bred prior to 1819.

Hyppolyte A tall, vigorous shrub of 1.5m / 5ft in height, with few thorns and small dark green leaves. The flowers, too, are small, flat at first, later reflexing into a ball-like formation. The colour is mauve-violet. Bred by Parmentier prior to 1842.

Ipsilante ('Ypsilante') A most beautiful rose, producing some of the finest blooms in this group. They are large, of a lustrous warm pink colouring, cupped at first, opening flat and quartered. The growth is shapely with fine foliage, and in my garden it is more disease resistant than any other Old Rose. Rich fragrance. Height 1.2m / 4ft. Bred by Vibert in 1821.

*Facing page, **Ipsilante** produces some of the finest blooms in this group: large, lustrous warm pink, cupped at first, opening flat and quartered*

*The mauve-violet flowers of **Hyppolyte** are flat at first, later reflexing into a ball-like formation*

The lilac-pink flowers of
Nestor *gradually take*
on mauve and grey tints

Facing page, ***Président***
de Sèze *bears attractive*
lilac buds that open to
magnificent large flowers
displaying a bewildering
array of tints

Nestor Lilac-pink flowers, deepening towards the centre, opening cupped, later becoming flat and quartered and gradually taking on mauve and grey tints. It has almost thornless growth of 1.2m / 4ft in height. Slightly fragrant. Introduced by Vibert 1834.

Pompon Panaché A pretty little miniature-flowered rose with neatly-formed blooms that have deep pink stripes on a cream ground. They are held in ones and twos on wiry upright stems with small leaves. Erect growth of 1–1.2m / 3–4ft in height. It has a strong and positively delicious fragrance. Bred by Moreau & Robert (France).

Président de Sèze ('Jenny Duval') A perfect bloom of this rose can be more beautiful than any other to be found among the Gallicas. Its attractive lilac buds open to magnificent large full-petalled flowers that display a bewildering array of tints. Graham Thomas mentions cerise, magenta, purple, violet, lilac-grey, soft brown and lilac-white, and all these colours are to be found, depending on the stage of development of the flower and the prevailing weather conditions. Perhaps it is simpler to say the overall colour effect is lilac, violet and silvery grey. It forms a sturdy shrub with ample foliage, and will grow to about 1.2m / 4ft in height. For some years a rose named 'Jenny Duval' was distributed by nurserymen,

including ourselves, but it is now generally agreed that this is the same as 'Président de Sèze'. To those who have known this rose under both names, it may seem strange that we have taken so long to arrive at this conclusion. My only defence is that this rose is so various and ever-changing in its colour that the confusion between the two was understandable. I have had more than one experienced rose enthusiast come to me with what they thought was yet another entirely different sport, and this too has turned out to be the same variety. The truth is that 'Président de Sèze' differs so widely according to the conditions under which it is grown that it seldom looks the same on any two occasions. There is a pleasing fragrance. Hébert (France) 1828.

***Surpasse Tout** has large, full, tightly packed flowers of light rose-crimson, turning with age to cerise-pink*

Sissinghurst Castle ('Rose des Maures') It is said that Vita Sackville-West and Harold Nicolson found this rose when they were clearing the garden of Sissinghurst Castle. The petals are a beautiful rich plum colour, edged and flecked with light magenta-crimson, and contrast strongly with the golden yellow stamens in the centre. It is a particularly tough rose and a great survivor and, when planted deeply, will sucker freely and form a thicket of upright stems. Lightly fragrant. Height 1.2m / 4ft. Reintroduced by V. Sackville-West (UK) 1947.

Surpasse Tout Large full, tightly packed flowers of light rose-crimson, turning with age to cerise-pink. The petals reflex and there is a button eye at the centre. The growth is strong and bushy, the height about 1.2m / 4ft. Strong fragrance. Bred by Hardy (France) 1823.

Said to originate from Vita Sackville-West's garden, **Sissinghurst Castle** *is a particularly tough rose and a great survivor*

With short but vigorous growth, ***Tricolore de Flandre*** *boasts fairly full white flowers heavily striped with lilac, purple and crimson*

Tricolore de Flandre Large, fairly full white flowers heavily striped with shades of lilac, purple and crimson. The growth is short, about 1m / 3ft in height, but vigorous with plentiful smooth foliage. Fragrant. Bred by Van Houtte (Belgium) 1846.

Tuscany A rose which can be compared with *R. gallica* var. *officinalis* and *Rosa Mundi*, both in its habit of growth and for its excellence as a garden shrub. It has fairly large semi-double flowers of the darkest maroon-crimson; these open wide, with bright golden stamens lighting up the centre. It forms a sturdy bush of 1.2m / 4ft and, on its own roots, will spread freely if permitted. The foliage is dark green. We do not know the age of this beautiful variety, but it probably goes back a very long way. There is only a slight fragrance. It was once known as the 'Old Velvet Rose' — the herbalist Gerard, writing in 1597, mentions a 'Velvet Rose', and it is likely that this is the same variety.

Tuscany Superb A larger version of 'Tuscany', with taller more vigorous growth to about 1.5m / 5ft, larger, more rounded leaves and larger flowers with more numerous petals. It is in fact 'more' everything, while remaining at the same time very similar in its general character and colouring; the stamens are partially obscured, as these tend to be hidden by the extra petals. It must have been either a sport or a seedling from 'Tuscany'—probably the latter. Bred by Rivers in 1837, it was one of the few Gallicas bred in Britain.

Tuscany Superb is a larger version of 'Tuscany', with taller more vigorous growth, larger, more rounded leaves and larger flowers with more numerous petals

***Violacea** has the appearance of a very old rose, although it is thought to originate from France about 1810*

Violacea ('La Belle Sultane') With its almost single flowers, this has the appearance of a very old rose, although it is thought to originate from France about 1810. The flowers are of the most wonderful rich darkest crimson, darker towards the edges and redder towards the centre. In the middle there is a big, bold group of golden stamens. It is a rather tall and wiry shrub and, while not particularly free flowering, it is well worth planting, especially with perennials in a mixed border. It is lightly fragrant. Height, 1.5–2m / 5–7ft. Introduced by Du Pont (France) before 1811.

Damask Roses

The Damask Rose, like the Gallica, dates back to ancient times. It is said to have been widely grown by the Persians, from whose country it spread to the Holy Land and other areas of the Middle East, eventually being brought to Europe by the Crusaders. S.F. Hamble gives the credit for this to Robert de Brie who, he says, brought the rose to his castle in Champagne at some time between 1254 and 1276, whence it was distributed throughout France and later brought to the British Isles.

According to Dr Hurst, the Damask Rose originated from a natural hybrid of the Gallica Rose and a wild species known as *Rosa phoenicea*. However, DNA analysis now strongly suggests that the original seed parent was a cross between *R. moschata* and *R. fedtschenkoana*, while the pollen parent was *R. gallica*. We thus have two widely differing parents, and it is therefore not surprising that this family is itself somewhat diverse in its nature.

In general Damask Roses are taller than Gallicas, perhaps 1.5m / 5ft in height, more lax in growth, with more and larger thorns. The leaves are elongated and pointed, of a greyish-green colour and downy on the underside. Where there are hips these will usually be long and thin. The flowers are nearly always a lovely clear pink and are often held in nicely poised sprays. They are usually strongly fragrant, the very name being synonymous with this quality. The Damasks bring elegance to the rose, both in leaf and general habit of growth.

Closely related to these roses is the Autumn Damask — *Rosa* × *damascena* var. *semperflorens*. This is a rose of great antiquity. It is not, perhaps, of the highest value for the garden, but is of great interest to those who study roses because it was the only rose to have the ability to repeat flower prior to the introduction of the China Rose late in the eighteenth century. It is of equal interest for its very long history. Dr Hurst tells us that it is first noted in the Greek island of Samos towards the end of the tenth century BC, where it was used in the cult of Aphrodite. It was later introduced to mainland Greece and then to Rome where it continued to play a part in ceremonies connected with Venus. In the first century BC Virgil, in *The Georgics*, mentions the rose which flowers twice a year, and this was no doubt the Autumn Damask. This is a rather prickly shrub, with the leaves running right up to, and clustering around, the flowers. It has an unsophisticated charm and the typical Damask fragrance. It eventually led to the Portland Roses, through which it played an important part in the development of repeat-flowering roses.

Celsiana A typical Damask Rose, with fine, graceful grey-green foliage. The flowers are large, opening wide, semi-double, and of a soft pink colour that later fades to blush, with a central boss of golden stamens. They are held in delicately poised sprays, and the petals have the appearance of crumpled silk. There is a strong fragrance. Height approximately 1.5m / 5ft. I place this rose high on any list of Old Roses. Known to have been in existence before 1750.

R.* × *damascena* var. *semperflorens (Autumn Damask, *Rosa damascena bifera*, 'Quatre Saisons', 'Rose of the Four Seasons') This is the repeat-flowering Autumn Damask I mentioned on the previous page. The flowers are clear pink, loosely double, with long sepals and a powerful and most delicious fragrance. It has rather spreading growth and greyish-green foliage. An ancient and most historic rose. Interestingly it sometimes sports to 'Quatre Saisons Blanc Mousseux' which, as the name suggests, is pure white with abundant mossy growth and repeat-flowers just as well as its parent. Height 1.5m / 5ft.

*Facing page, **Celsiana** is a typical Damask Rose, its soft pink flowers are large, opening wide, semi-double, and held in delicately poised sprays*

R. × damascena var. semperflor-ens *Autumn Damask* *is an ancient and most historic rose but has the ability to repeat flower well*

R. × damascena
Versicolor *carries its*
semi-double flowers with
elegance in dainty, open
sprays

***R. × damascena* Versicolor** ('York and Lancaster') A tall shrub with clear, downy grey-green foliage, which carries its flowers with elegance in dainty, open sprays. These are unusual in that they may be pink or almost white, or a mixture of both, the white being flecked with pink and vice versa, all these variations being found on one shrub at the same time. The individual flowers are informal and semi-double, usually exposing their stamens. It is not a dramatic shrub, but it does have a certain airy elegance. The story that the two factions in the Wars of the Roses each took a bloom from a bush of this rose—a red and a white—is probably not true. The roses of the two houses were more likely to have been

R. gallica officinalis and *R. alba semi-plena*, but there is no firm historical evidence for this. It is important to obtain bushes from correct stock, as the flowers can revert to pink. Strongly fragrant. Height 1.5m / 5ft. Known to be in existence before 1550.

Gloire de Guilan In 1949 Nancy Lindsay collected this rose from Iran, where it is used for the making of attar of roses. It forms a loose sprawling shrub with apple-green leaves. The flowers are cupped at first, later becoming flat and quartered. Their colour is a pink of unusual clarity and purity, and they are very fragrant although always much more strongly so in warmer climates. I have found it to be particularly resistant to disease. Height 1.2m / 4ft.

*The highly fragrant blooms of **Gloire de Guilan** are of a pink of unusual purity and clarity*

The red-tipped petals of **Hebe's Lip** *give this rose its name*

*Facing page, **Ispahan** flowers early and continues over a long period, bearing blooms that are large and very full, opening flat, and of a rich warm pink that does not fade*

Hebe's Lip (Rubrotincta) A modest rose but not without its attractions. It has cupped, semi-double flowers, with red-tipped petals that give it its name. A strong and myrrh-like fragrance. The growth is short and thorny with fresh green foliage. Height 1.2m / 4ft. It is probably of hybrid origin, perhaps Damask × *Rosa arvensis*. Bred by Lee (UK) 1846.

Ispahan ('Pompon des Princes') A very fine shrub which begins to flower early and continues over a long period. The flowers are large and very full, opening flat, and of a rich warm pink that does not fade. A good cut flower, lasting well in water. It has a glorious fragrance. Height 1.5m / 5ft. In cultivation before 1832.

*Also known as the 'Painted Damask', the flowers of **Leda** become stained with pink at the rim as they open*

*Facing page, **La Ville de Bruxelles** bears exceptionally large full-petalled blooms of a clear rich pink. When fully open the petals reflex at the edges, leaving a slightly domed centre filled with small petals*

La Ville de Bruxelles ('Ville de Bruxelles') Exceptionally large full-petalled blooms of a clear rich pink. When fully open the petals reflex at the edges, leaving a slightly domed centre filled with small petals. A truly luxurious flower of fine quality. The foliage is large and plentiful, pale green in colour and of typical Damask shapeliness. Its growth is upright but often weighed down by the heavy blooms, particularly in moist weather. Rich fragrance. Height 1.2m / 4ft or more if lightly pruned. Vibert (France) 1836.

Leda Milk-white flowers with the slightest suggestion of pink. As they open they develop a picot effect, the rim of the petals becoming stained with crimson, so giving rise to its other name the 'Painted Damask'. The blooms are full petalled, reflexing to reveal a button centre. Although not perhaps quite so exciting as the description implies, it is a pretty rose with good foliage. Slight fragrance. Height 1m / 3ft. Prior to 1827.

Madame Hardy is one of the classic Old Roses—few others approach the perfection of its compact flowers

Madame Hardy One of the classic Old Roses—few others approach the perfection of its flowers. They are not very large, of pretty cupped formation at first, later becoming flat and finally reflexing. There is the slightest hint of blush in the early stages, but later they become a pure glistening white, while at the centre a small green eye adds to the attraction. They are held in nicely poised clusters, and are fragrant with just a hint of lemon. It will grow to about 1.5m / 5ft and is reasonably strong, but it will repay generous treatment with manure. The foliage is pale green. We cannot be sure of its origin, though it is obviously not pure Damask, the leaves and growth showing signs

of Centifolia influence. It is strongly fragrant. Bred in 1832 by Hardy (who had charge of the Empress Josephine's famous rose collection at Malmaison) and named after his wife.

Madame Zöetmans A charming rose not often seen but gaining in popularity. Its flowers are of medium size, fully double, of cupped formation at first, opening to reveal a button eye. Their colour is white, tinted with blush at the centre, and they are borne on graceful growth on a nice bushy plant with fresh green foliage. Strongly fragrant. Height 1.2m / 4ft. Bred by Marest (France) 1830.

*Not often seen until recently, the white-flowered **Madame Zöetmans** is now gaining in popularity*

Marie Louise is a lax-growing shrub with unusually large deep pink flowers, the petals reflexing, and very fragrant. The sheer weight and quantity of the flowers often bows the branches down to the ground

Marie Louise A lax-growing shrub vying with 'La Ville de Bruxelles' for the splendour of its flowers. These are unusually large and full, of deep pink with the petals reflexing, and very fragrant. The sheer weight and quantity of the flowers often bows down the branches to the ground. The height is about 1.2m / 4ft with plentiful large foliage. Here we have a rose that might well be encouraged to flop over a low retaining wall. Raised at Malmaison, 1813.

Oeillet Parfait A compact, twiggy shrub of 1–1.2m / 3–4ft, with small pale green leaves. The flowers open flat with numerous petals of warm pink colouring, later reflexing almost to a ball. There is also a striped Gallica of the same name.

Omar Khayyám This rose is perhaps of more historic interest than garden value. It is the rose that grows on the poet Edward Fitzgerald's grave at Boulge, Suffolk, and which was itself first raised from seed from a rose on Omar Khayyam's grave at Nishapur in Iran. The flowers are soft pink, fragrant, of medium size, and quartered, with a button eye. The foliage is grey-green and downy. Height 1m / 3ft. About 1893.

The warm pink flowers of **Oeillet Parfait** *open flat, with the petals later reflexing almost to a ball*

Petite Lisette A miniature-flowered Damask carrying small bunches of perfect little flowers, each well filled with clear pink petals. It has small, neat, downy grey-green foliage, and forms an excellent well-rounded shrub of 1–1.2m / 3–4ft in height. Fragrant. Bred and introduced by Vibert (France) 1817.

Professeur Emile Perrot ('Kazanlik', *Rosa damascena* 'Trigintipetala') With 'Trigintipetala' and 'Gloire de Guilan', this is one of several roses traditionally sold under the single name of 'Kazanlik'. They are all grown at Kazanlik in Bulgaria for the production of attar of roses. The blooms of 'Professeur Emile Perrot' are pink and of no great merit, but it does form a graceful and typical Damask shrub and has, as might be expected, a rich fragrance, especially in hot summers. Height 1.5–1.8m / 5–6ft. Probably of great antiquity.

Quatre Saisons see *R.* × *damascena* var. *semperflorens*.

Saint Nicholas A recent addition to this very old class, which occurred as a chance seedling, in 1950, in the garden of The Hon. Robert James, at Richmond, Yorkshire. The flowers are semi-double, opening flat, and of a rich pink colour with yellow stamens. It forms a short prickly bush of 1.5m / 5ft in height, with good, dark green foliage.

*Facing page, **Petite Lisette** is a miniature-flowered Damask carrying small bunches of perfect little flowers, each well filled with clear pink petals*

*The result of a chance seedling, **Saint Nicholas** has semi-double flowers of a rich pink with yellow stamens*

Alba Roses

The Alba Roses form another very old group. In existence in classical times and probably brought to Britain by the Romans, they were widely grown in the Middle Ages, no doubt mainly for medicinal purposes, and appear in many paintings of that period. The other classes of ancient roses have a great deal in common and a casual observer might see them as all of one type, but this is not the case with the Albas which are quite distinct. It is generally agreed that they are the result of natural hybridization between the Damask Rose and *Rosa canina*, the Dog Rose of our hedgerows, or at least a species closely allied to it. A cursory inspection of the growth of the Dog Rose will show its close affinity to Alba Roses. As with other Old Roses many of its varieties appear to be the result of further hybridization with roses of other classes.

The Albas form a small but important group which includes some of the best and most beautiful of the Old Roses. Their growth is larger than that of the other old classes, often 1.8m / 6ft or more in height, and it is no doubt for this reason that they were formerly known as Tree Roses. The flowers, as the name suggests, are rather limited in their colour range, being restricted to white, blush and pink, but they have a delicacy and refinement that is hard to match elsewhere. Their foliage is frequently grey-green in colour, and this tones well with their soft tints and provides an excellent contrast with other roses and plants. They are generally extremely healthy although some varieties suffer from rust; this doesn't seem to worry them much. They nearly all have a pleasing and characteristic fragrance.

The delicate appearance of the flowers is in sharp contrast to the undoubted toughness of the plant which will grow under difficult conditions. Albas are, in fact, among the most easily grown of all roses, and even in partial shade will do better than most others, although no roses really like such conditions. Whenever we are asked at our nursery for roses that will grow in partial shade, it is always to these we first turn. They are ideal for the border or as individual specimens, or for planting in the wilder areas of the garden. They also make perfect hosts for the late-flowering varieties of *Clematis viticella*. They will also form a particularly fine hedge, different varieties of similar stature mingling together most satisfactorily. The taller varieties may be trained as climbers and they are quite happy when grown on a north wall.

*Facing page, **Alba Maxima** is an ancient rose known to have existed in classical times, with fully double flowers that are blush-pink at first but soon turn to creamy-white*

R. × *alba* Alba Maxima ('Great Double White', 'Cheshire Rose', 'Jacobite Rose') An ancient rose known to have existed in classical times, it has been grown in cottage gardens in Britain for many centuries, where it lives on almost indefinitely, continually renewing its growth. It is not uncommon to see this variety growing, apparently wild, in hedgerows, such plants marking the place where a cottage once stood but has long since gone. There can be no

better testimony to its durability. Surely this must be one of the longest lived of all roses? It forms a tall if rather top-heavy shrub of 1.8m / 6ft, and although the individual flowers are not particularly distinguished, they are most effective in the mass. Fully double, they are blush-pink at first, but, soon turn to creamy-white. Strong fragrance.

R. × *alba* Alba Semiplena Said to have been the 'White Rose of York', this is a luxuriant shrub with fine grey-green foliage and elegant shapely growth. The flowers are large, almost single, symmetrical in outline and milky-white in colour, with a large boss of stamens. They are followed in the autumn by large orange Dog Rose hips. This is one of the roses cultivated at Kazanlik, Bulgaria, for the production of attar of roses. In every way a first class garden shrub. Very fragrant. Height 1.8m / 6ft. A very ancient rose which can be traced back to the fourteenth century.

Amélia Here we have a smaller shrub than is usual among Albas. It bears large, strongly fragrant, pure pink semi-double flowers with pronounced golden stamens. Its height is about 1.2m / 4ft. Bred by Vibert (France) 1823.

Amélia is smaller than other Albas and bears large, pure pink semi-double flowers

Facing page, **R × alba Alba Semiplena** *bears large flowers, almost single, with a large boss of stamens, followed in the autumn by large orange Dog Rose hips*

*The semi-double, slightly cupped flowers of **Belle Amour** are of a soft salmon-pink - a shade almost unique among Old Roses*

Belle Amour A strong shrub, 1.8m / 6ft in height, bearing clusters of semi-double, slightly cupped flowers of a soft salmon-pink—a shade almost unique among Old Roses. These have a myrrh fragrance which suggests this rose may have some Ayrshire 'Splendens' in its make up. It was originally discovered growing on the wall of a convent at Elboeuf, Normandy, France.

Céleste ('Celestial') A modest rose, much treasured for the charm and delicacy of its exquisitely scrolled buds and semi-double flowers of lovely soft pink colouring. These are not large and have yellow stamens. The blooms are beautiful against the grey-green of the typically Alba foliage, and have a sweet fragrance. However the growth is anything but delicate, forming a robust shrub which, in our experience, should not be pruned too severely, otherwise it tends to make growth at the expense of flowers. It forms a shrub of 1.5m / 5ft in height by 1.2m / 4ft across. It is said to have been bred in Holland towards the end of the eighteenth century.

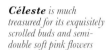

Céleste is much treasured for its exquisitely scrolled buds and semi-double soft pink flowers

Félicité Parmentier
bears perfect quartered flowers tightly packed with petals of clear fresh pink; these later reflex and fade to cream at the edges

Félicité Parmentier At its best this is a most beautiful rose, with perfect quartered flowers very tightly packed with petals of clear fresh pink; these later reflex and fade to cream at the edges. The growth is quite short, about 1.2m / 4ft in height, but bushy, with many thorns and pale green leaves. It is an excellent rose, but in dry seasons on sandy soil the flowers sometimes fail to open properly; with good management this should not be a problem. Very fragrant. Bred by Parmentier in 1834.

Madame Legras de Saint Germain A rose of exceptional beauty. Starting as a prettily cupped bud, it opens to form a perfectly shaped, slightly domed flower with many petals. The colour is a glowing white with just a tinge of yellow, and this gives us a hint as to its origins—there has to have been a Noisette somewhere in its breeding. It would be hard to think of a more perfect marriage than Alba and Noisette, although in this case it has led to one weakness: the flowers can be damaged by wet weather. Otherwise it is sheer perfection. The growth is tall and lax, forming a graceful shrub of 1.8m / 6ft in height, with very few thorns and pale green leaves. Strong and delicious fragrance. It can equally well be grown as a climber. Introduced prior to 1848.

The exceptionally beautiful **Madame Legras de Saint Germain** *has Noisette in its breeding, lending its glowing white blooms a slight tinge of yellow*

Madame Plantier
*forms a sprawling mass of
graceful growth with
clusters of pompom-like
blooms and is equally
effective when trained as a
climber*

Madame Plantier This is an Alba / Noisette hybrid and, in fact, is sometimes classified as a Noisette. It forms a sprawling mound of graceful growth covered with large clusters of rather small pompon-like blooms against pale green foliage. The colour is creamy-white, lightly tinged with yellow at first, later turning to pure white, and there is a pointed green eye at the centre of each flower. Its sweet and powerful fragrance fills the air. It is equally effective when trained as a climber, and I have vivid memories of a visit to Sissinghurst Castle and being shown this rose climbing up the trunks of fruit trees where they made a wonderful sight like billowing dresses. The height is 1.8m / 6ft spreading to 1.8m / 6ft across. Bred and introduced by Plantier (France) 1835.

Maiden's Blush ('Great Maiden's Blush', known in France as 'Cuisse de Nymphe Émue' and at other times and in various countries as 'La Royale', 'La Seduisante', 'Virginale', 'Incarnata') This forms a graceful arching shrub of 1.5m / 5ft in height with typical grey-green Alba foliage. The flowers are loosely double, of soft blush-pink, the petals reflexing slightly with age and paling towards the edges. They have a wonderful fragrance. An old and much loved rose and certainly in existence before the beginning of the sixteenth century.

Maiden's Blush (small) This has smaller flowers than its larger cousin and grows to only 1.2m / 4ft in height. I do not know whether it was a sport or a seedling from 'Maiden's Blush', but it is similar in every respect except size. Raised at Kew in 1797.

A graceful arching shrub with typical grey-green Alba foliage, **Maiden's Blush** *bears blush-pink blooms with petals that reflex and pale towards the edges with age*

The unusual flowers of **Pompon Blanc Parfait** *appear late in the season and are then produced a few at a time in long succession*

Facing page, **Queen of Denmark** *bears full, perfectly quartered flowers with a button eye and a particularly strong Old Rose fragrance*

Pompon Blanc Parfait An unusual rose and difficult to compare with any other. It has little round buds which open to small, flat, tightly-packed pompon flowers on short thin stems. The flowers are pale lilac-pink in colour and of very neat formation. They appear late in the season and are then produced a few at a time in long succession. The growth tends to be slow to develop, with small grey-green leaves and twiggy, rather stiff, almost reluctant growth of perhaps 1.2m / 4ft in height. Slight fragrance. Introduced 1876.

Queen of Denmark ('Königin von Dänemark') Few old roses can equal this for the perfection of its individual blooms. These are prettily cupped in the bud and later develop into a full perfectly quartered, slightly reflexing flower with a button eye at the centre. The colour is a warm rose-pink. A particularly strong and delicious Old Rose fragrance. The growth is comparatively short, perhaps 1.2 or 1.5m / 4 or 5ft in height, with typical grey-green foliage. Like all Albas it is easily grown, but superb blooms can be obtained with good cultivation. Raised in 1816 by John Booth, who recorded it as a seedling from 'Maiden's Blush', and introduced it in 1826.

Centifolia Roses

The Centifolias were for a long time thought to be the most ancient of all roses, but subsequent research has proved this to be far from the truth. They are mere children by comparison with the three classes discussed so far. It seems that they evolved over a period extending from early in the seventeenth century to the beginning of the eighteenth century, that they were largely the result of the work of Dutch breeders, and that during this period some two hundred varieties were known to have been introduced. It is not easy to say exactly how they arose, but Dr Hurst's work shows that *Rosa gallica*, *R. phoenicea*, *R. moschata* and *R. canina* all come into their make-up. This would seem to indicate that a Damask / Alba cross might have occurred at some time, although it was probably rather more complex than that and preliminary DNA analysis suggests a close affinity with the Damasks but not the Albas. It is likely that a series of crosses took place over a long period, resulting in what came to be regarded as a distinct breed. Centifolias were great favourites with our forefathers who seem to have prized them above all others, and evidence of this is provided by the Dutch and Flemish flower painters who used them in their work more frequently than any other roses.

The typical Centifolia has lax, open, rather lanky growth with a mixture of large and small thorns; the leaves are large, rounded and broadly toothed; the flowers tend to be heavy and globular with numerous petals. In spite of all this, Centifolias are seldom clumsy and their luxuriant blooms nod gracefully on their stems. Their colours are, in the main, warm clear shades of pink, which do not normally fade in the sun. There are also a number of varieties of hybrid origin which tend towards crimson and pleasing shades of purple and mauve, as well as one or two whites. They are rightly famous for their rich fragrance.

The Centifolias have a strong tendency to produce sports, and this has resulted in a number of unusual forms. Foremost amongst these are the Moss Roses, but there are also quaint and unusual varieties such as 'Chapeau de Napoléon', 'Bullata' and a number of charming miniatures.

It is sometimes worthwhile giving some of the more lax-growing varieties a little support to stop them bending too near the ground. Pruning can be rather more severe than with other Old Roses, and should be just enough to keep the bush in order, without losing the grace of their arching growth.

Blanchefleur Heavy, full-petalled, creamy-white flowers with a tinge of blush at the centre and red on the tips of the petals. It forms a vigorous 1.5m / 5ft bush with many thorns and apple-green foliage, and shows signs of hybrid origin. Perhaps a little coarse in appearance for my taste, but as a white Centifolia it is valuable. Fragrant. Raised by Vibert (France) 1835.

Bullata ('Lettuce-leaved Rose') This is probably a sport of 'Centifolia' to which it is similar, with the same cupped flowers and rich fragrance. The difference lies in the leaves, which are excessively enlarged and deeply crinkled, like the leaves of a lettuce. It is perhaps due to the effort of producing such foliage that the flowers tend to be rather inferior to 'Centifolia' and do not always open well. The height is 1.2m / 4ft. An interesting curiosity that seems to have originated in 1801.

R. × centifolia ('Cabbage Rose', 'Rose of a Hundred Leaves', 'Rose des Peintres', 'Provence Rose') The type from which this group derives its name. Even those who know little or nothing about Old Roses will usually have heard of it by its name of 'Old Cabbage Rose'. To the old herbalists it was the 'Queen of Roses', and indeed it is the most beautiful of the Centifolia Roses with its heavy nodding blooms of warm glowing pink and rich Old Rose fragrance. It has strong, nicely arching growth of about 1.5m / 5ft. The flowers are at their best in warm, dry weather. Prior to 1600.

***R. × centifolia* Spong** A miniature Centifolia of bushy, branching growth, about 1.2m / 4ft in height, with typical Centifolia leaves. Its flowers are rich pink, paling a little towards the edges. It is rather less formal than 'De Meaux' and 'Petite de Hollande', and has the bad habit of holding its petals long after the flower has died, which is rather unsightly. This is a pretty little rose, but the least effective of the miniatures. Raised by Spong (England), introduced 1805.

***Blanchefleur**, with its heavy, full-petalled flowers forms a vigorous bush with apple-green foliage and many thorns*

R. × centifolia Unique *has petals with a lovely silky texture and a good fragrance*

Facing page, **Chapeau de Napoléon** *is very similar to* R. × centifolia, *but distinguished by the greatly enlarged calyx which gives the bud the appearance of a three-cornered cockade hat*

R. × centifolia Unique ('Unique Blanche', 'White Provence Unique') Creamy-white flowers which are nicely cupped at first, later opening rather untidily with a button eye. At their best they can be most beautiful, the petals having a lovely silky texture. It has strong (if rather untidy) growth and there is a good fragrance. Height 1.2m / 4ft. Discovered at Needham, Suffolk, 1775.

Chapeau de Napoléon (*R. × centifolia* 'Cristata', 'Crested Moss') This rose is very similar to *R. × centifolia*, described above. It is distinguished by the fact that the calyx is greatly enlarged in much the same way as a Moss Rose, giving the bud the appearance of a three-cornered cockade hat. Closer observation will reveal that this is not the same as the 'moss' of a Moss Rose, but what Bunyard describes as 'an exaggerated development of the sepals'. However we describe it, the result is very attractive. Although the open flower is not quite so deep as *R. × centifolia*, it is otherwise indistinguishable, with the same clear pink colouring. It is said that it was originally found in 1820, growing in the crevice of an old wall at Fribourg in Switzerland. This suggests, rather surprisingly, that it was a seedling, not a sport. There is a rich fragrance. Height about 1.5m / 5ft. Introduced by Vibert (France) as 'Crested Moss', 1826.

Also known by many other names, **Cottage Maid** *bears many-petalled flowers of a creamy-white, delicately striped with pale pink*

Facing page, **De Meaux** *is ideal for very small gardens: the flowers open as miniature cups and develop into small pompon flowers of typical Old Rose pink*

Cottage Maid A rose which has been known by many names in its time: 'Belle des Jardins', 'La Rubanée', 'Village Maid', 'Panachée à Fleurs Doubles', 'La Belle Villageoise', 'Dometil Beccard' and 'Dominic Boccardo'. It is perhaps more properly known as 'Variegata', but we have chosen 'Cottage Maid' as being rather more picturesque. The flowers are quite large and globular in shape with numerous petals, the colour creamy-white, delicately striped with pale pink. It is a vigorous bushy shrub of 1.5m / 5ft in height, with dark green foliage and many thorns. Rich fragrance. Introduced by Vibert (France) 1845.

De Meaux ('Rose de Meaux') A miniature Centifolia which has to be compared with other miniatures of this class—'Petite de Hollande' and 'Spong'. Each of these is charming in its own way, like the little roses we might expect to see decorating tea cups. They are ideal for very small gardens. In spite of some reports to the contrary, I suspect that they are all sports of larger Centifolias. 'De Meaux' forms a bushy, twiggy shrub of 1.1m / 3½ft in height, with tiny flowers of only a little more than 25mm / 1in across, and small light green foliage to match. The flowers open as little miniature cups and develop into small pompon flowers of typical Old Rose pink. It is in every way a charming little shrub. Said to have originated with a man named Sweet in 1789.

*Fantin-Latour bears
flowers of a nicely cupped
shape, the outer petals
reflexing as the flower ages
to reveal a button centre*

Fantin-Latour This rose turned up as a seedling in an English garden in 1940 and is clearly not of pure Centifolia descent. The leaves and growth show signs of China Rose influence. The flowers, however, have much of the character of a Centifolia, being of a nicely cupped shape, the outer petals reflexing as the flower ages to reveal a button centre. The colour is a blush-pink which deepens towards the centre and there is a delicate and pleasing fragrance. It forms an excellent shrub with good broad growth of 1.5m / 5ft in height although it is rather susceptible to blackspot. Named, most appropriately, after the great French artist Henri Fantin-Latour, whose finest paintings were nearly all of flowers and whose favourite flower was the rose. In every way a fine shrub.

Juno Like 'Fantin-Latour', this rose has more modern affinities and is probably connected with the Bourbons. It bears fragrant globular flowers of soft blush pink, later opening flat to reveal a button eye. The growth is rather lax and about 1.2m / 4ft in height. In cultivation before 1832.

Paul Ricault This is a 1.5m / 5ft shrub of medium vigour. The flowers are deep pink, very full petalled and rather globular, the outer petals later recurving. It has a strong fragrance and is free flowering, the blooms hanging gracefully upon the stem. It is sometimes classed as a Hybrid China and sometimes as a Hybrid Perpetual. Raised by Portemer (France) 1845.

*Probably connected to the Bourbons, **Juno** bears fragrant globular flowers of soft blush pink, later opening flat to reveal a button eye*

Petite de Hollande
is a pretty miniature, with
charming little Centifolia
flowers of pure rose-pink.

Petite de Hollande ('Petite Junon de Hollande', 'Pompon des Dames', 'Normandica') This is another pretty miniature, with charming little Centifolia flowers of pure rose-pink. It forms a nice bushy little shrub of 1.2m / 4ft with small leaves and tiny flowers all to scale. Although all are delightful, it is perhaps the best of the miniature-flowered Centifolias, and there is very little to choose between it and 'De Meaux'. Fragrant. First raised in Holland about 1800.

Robert de Diable A lax shrub with dark green leaves and thorny stems. The flowers are purple, shaded with slate-grey and splashed with carmine, providing a most pleasing mixture of colour, particularly in hot weather. Of neat rosette shape, the blooms are not large, the petals reflexing towards the edges. Both foliage and flowers show signs of Gallica influence. Late flowering. Introduced about 1831. Height 1.2m / 4ft.

The Bishop ('Le Rosier Évêque') A very double flower of rosette formation and unique colouring: cerise-magenta with pale lilac on the reverse of the petals, later becoming slate-grey and Parma-violet. In certain lights the blooms appear to be almost blue. Gallica influence is very much in evidence. Fragrant. It has rather erect growth of 1.8m / 6ft in height. In cultivation about 1831.

*The uniquely coloured very double flowers of **The Bishop** can appear almost blue in certain lights*

Tour de Malakoff A most beautiful rose which will appeal to those who like the purple shades. The flowers are large, opening wide and slightly cupped and only loosely double, but it is the colouring which is their chief glory—a purplish-crimson tinted with magenta becoming violet and with a few stamens usually to be seen at the centre. It is magnificent at all stages. The growth is excellent, perhaps 1.8m / 6ft in height, arching broadly to form a rather sprawling shrub although it is rather susceptible to blackspot. Given suitable support it might well be used as a climber. Raised by Soupert & Notting (Luxemburg) 1856.

White de Meaux This is a white sport from 'De Meaux', to which it is similar in every way except that the flowers are white tinged with pink. This may sound attractive, but unfortunately the pink is such that it gives the flowers a rather dirty appearance. It is, nonetheless, worthy of its place.

Moss Roses

The Moss Roses are Centifolias and Damasks which have developed moss-like growth on their sepals and, in some varieties, a little way down the flower stem. This peculiarity is the result of a sport, or fault, in the plant. Small glandular growth is always present to some extent on the sepals of the flower, and in the case of Moss Roses this has become greatly exaggerated. The result is that the bud is covered in this mossy material, giving a most charming effect. It is quite sticky to the touch and aromatic too. We do not know exactly when this curious phenomenon occurred, but Dr Hurst quotes various French sources which state that a rose of this nature existed in France at Carcassonne in 1696, where it had been for half a century, having been first brought there by one Freard Ducastel. The earliest mention of it in England was in 1724, when it was listed in the catalogue of Robert Furber of Kensington. Mossing has probably occurred from time to time before and since; indeed it has been recorded subsequently on at least three other occasions. It has also occurred on an Autumn Damask, giving us the 'Perpetual White Moss'.

The majority of Moss Roses were bred over a short period of time, from approximately 1850 to 1870. Arriving, as they did, comparatively late on the rose scene, they show considerable signs of hybridity; in some varieties there are definite signs of China Rose ancestry and indeed some of them repeat flower really quite well. Here we have the first hint of the Modern Rose creeping in on the Old. The result is sometimes a loss of that charm which we so value in Old Roses, the first loss of innocence. Nonetheless, most Moss Roses have a beauty which is different from that of other roses. A Moss Rose bud just opening does have a certain charm that is all its own—in George Bunyard's words, 'a cosiness'; for, as he says, 'cosiness lay at the very centre of Victorian taste'. Indeed, I doubt that any other age would have taken them up quite so enthusiastically. They are often a little more stiff and upright than Centifolias, and there is more variation in quality. Disease resistance is often rather suspect. It is at this stage in the development of the rose that we have to become a little more selective in our choice of varieties.

Most Moss Roses have inherited the strong fragrance of their Centifolia ancestors and pruning should be as recommended for the Centifolias.

Blanche Moreau Very double, paper-white flowers, starting as a cup and later becoming flat, with contrasting brown moss. This rose is said to be a cross between 'Comtesse de Murinais' and 'Quatre Saisons Blanc', and it does occasionally flower in the autumn. It is perhaps a little lacking in refinement. The growth is rather slender and tall, up to 1.8m / 6ft. Raised by Moreau-Robert (France) 1880.

Capitaine Basroger Rather shapeless flowers of cerise-purple, and fairly coarse and ungainly growth which is tall and narrow, about 1.8m / 6ft. Little moss. Raised by Moreau-Robert (France) 1890.

R. × centifolia Muscosa is probably the original Moss Rose from which the others are descended and none has excelled it

Capitaine John Ingram Full recurving flowers of dusky maroon-purple later becoming purple and showing a button eye. The buds are only sparsely covered with red moss. It forms a vigorous bushy shrub with dark foliage and many thorns. Fragrant. Height 1.5m / 5ft. Bred by Laffay (France) 1854.

***R.* × *centifolia* Muscosa** ('Old Pink Moss', 'Common Moss') It seems certain that this well-known rose was a sport from *Rosa centifolia*. It is a little smaller and less deep in the flower, probably due to the burden of producing moss. Otherwise it has the same warm, rich pink colouring and strong fragrance, as well as the elegance and poise and other good characteristics of its parent. This is probably the original Moss Rose from which the others are descended. Although many varieties have followed, none has excelled it, either for the beauty of its flowers or its value as a garden shrub. Height 1.2m / 4ft. It probably dates back to 1700.

***R.* × *centifolia* Shailer's White Moss** (*Rosa* × *centifolia* 'Muscosa Alba', 'Clifton Rose', also often known as 'White Bath') This is a sport from 'Old Pink Moss' and is similar except for its colour. As one might expect, it is a most attractive rose, with cupped white flowers tinted with blush at the centre when they first open. It is certainly the best white Moss Rose, and indeed one of the most beautiful of the small band of white Old Roses. It forms an excellent shrub of 1.2m / 4ft in height. Fragrant. Discovered by Shailer, 1788.

R. × centifolia
Shailer's White
Moss *bears lovely*
cupped white flowers
tinted blush at the centre
when they first open

Comtesse de Murinais Pretty blush-pink buds enfolded in hard green moss, opening to superb quartered blooms with a button eye and fading to white. The growth is vigorous, tall and erect, its many thorns and light green foliage suggesting a Damask ancestry. Height 1.8m / 6ft. Fragrant. A most beautiful rose. Bred by Vibert (France) 1843.

*The buds of **Capitaine John Ingram**, which are only sparsely covered with red moss, open to reveal full recurving flowers of dusky maroon-purple*

The well mossed buds of
**Duchesse de
Verneuil** *open into
frash pink flowers with
petals that are slightly
paler on the reverse side*

Duchesse de Verneuil A charming rose of delicate refinement, with flowers of a clear fresh-pink colouring, the petals being slightly paler on the reverse side. It has well mossed buds, good foliage and forms a shapely shrub of 1.2m / 4ft in height. Bred by Portemer (France), introduced 1856.

Général Kléber Pretty buds wrapped in fresh green moss opening to form wide flat flowers with silky petals of soft clear pink and a button eye at the centre. It has good bushy growth, about 1.2 × 1.2m / 4 × 4ft, with light green foliage. One of the most beautiful of the Moss Roses. Fragrant. Bred by Robert (France), introduced 1856.

Gloire des Mousseuses ('Madame Alboni') This variety has the largest flowers of the Moss Roses, and indeed some of the largest flowers of all Old Roses. Its full-petalled blooms open wide and flat, reflex at the edges and have a strong fragrance. Their colour is a soft pink which pales with age. There is ample pale green moss on unusually long sepals. A beautiful flower that may occasionally be damaged by rain. It forms a strong, rather erect, but not unshapely shrub of 1.5m / 5ft with thick stems and large, light green leaves. Bred by Laffay (France) 1852.

*Bearing some of the largest flowers of all Old Roses, **Gloire des Mousseuses** boasts ample pale green moss on unusually long sepals*

*The flowers of **Henri Martin** are held daintily on thin, wiry stems and are of an unusually pure crimson for a Moss Rose*

Henri Martin ('Red Moss') Long crimson buds with contrasting but rather sparse green moss. The open flower is not very full but has an attractive, neatly rounded form, and is of an unusually pure crimson for a Moss Rose, later becoming purple-crimson. The flowers, which are held daintily on thin, wiry stems on a vigorous shrub of up to 1.8m / 6ft in height, are followed by red hips. Fragrant. Bred by Laffay (France) 1863.

James Mitchell A vigorous shrub with small magenta flowers that fade to lilac-pink. The buds are dainty and wrapped in dark moss. Height 1.5m / 5ft. Bred by Verdier (France) 1861.

Japonica ('Moussu du Japon') This rose not only has mossy buds but also moss spreading heavily well down the stem, and even on to the leaves. The blooms are magenta-pink and not very impressive; the foliage has purple and copper tints when young. Really only valuable as a curiosity. Height 1m / 3ft.

Jeanne de Montfort A tall and vigorous Moss Rose of 1.8–2m / 6–7ft in height. Its flowers are clear pink, not very full, have exposed yellow stamens and are sweetly scented. The buds have plenty of brown moss on long sepals. Bred by Robert (France) 1851.

Little Gem A miniature variety which has small, flat, pompon flowers of a uniform light crimson, but with very little moss. It forms a low bush, no more than 0.6m / 2ft in height, with small leaves. Raised by Paul (England) 1880.

*The buds of **Jeanne de Montfort** have plenty of brown moss on long sepals, opening to clear pink flowers with exposed yellow stamens*

*The large cup-shaped flowers of **Louis Gimard** are tightly packed with petals of light crimson*

*Facing page, Free flowering with graceful growth, **Maréchal Davoust** bears light crimson blooms tinted with purple and mauve*

Louis Gimard Large cup-shaped flowers, tightly packed with petals of light crimson. It has deep green foliage and the buds are enclosed in dark moss. Height 1.5m / 5ft. Raised by Pernet Père (France) 1877.

Madame Delaroche-Lambert Attractive crimson buds with dark moss and long sepals, opening to form flat, shapely, full-petalled flowers of crimson-purple. It makes a good bushy shrub of 1.2m / 4ft in height and occasionally repeat flowers. Bred by Robert (France) 1851.

Maréchal Davoust One of the most satisfactory Moss Roses, when we consider it as a garden shrub. It flowers freely and has graceful, shapely, rather arching growth, creating a most pleasing overall effect. The buds are attractive, with green-brown moss, and open to form shapely flowers of light crimson tinted with purple and mauve, the petals reflexing to show a button centre and a green eye. Height about 1.2m / 4ft. Fragrant. Raised by Robert (France) 1853.

Mousseline This rose is often found under the name 'Alfred de Dalmas'. No other Moss Rose repeat flowers quite so well, except perhaps 'Salet', which is a much less attractive variety. The buds of 'Mousseline' are pretty and have green-brown moss, although this is not very plentiful. The open flowers are medium sized, cupped, of a soft flesh-pink and delicately scented. The growth is bushy, with pale green, peculiarly spoon-shaped leaves. It appears to be related to the Autumn Damask, probably 'Quatre Saisons Blanc'. A charming rose. Height 1.5m / 5ft. Raised by Portemer (France), introduced 1855.

Nuits de Young ('Old Black') The darkest of all the Moss Roses, having small flowers of rich velvety maroon-purple lit by contrasting yellow stamens, with thin buds wrapped in very dark moss. Its growth is slender and wiry and it has small, dark leaves of an almost purple shade. Careful thinning at pruning time and some feeding will be worthwhile. Height 1.5m / 5ft. Bred by Laffay (France) 1845.

René d'Anjou Pretty buds with brown-green moss opening to beautiful soft pink flowers with a delicious perfume. The foliage is tinted with bronze and it forms a bushy shrub of 1.2m / 4ft in height. A delightful rose. Bred by Robert (France) 1853.

*Facing page, **Nuits de Young**, the darkest of all the Moss Roses, has small flowers of rich velvety maroon-purple lit by contrasting yellow stamens, with dark leaves of an almost purple shade*

*The pretty buds of **Mousseline** have green-brown moss and no other Moss Rose repeat flowers quite so well - with the exception of 'Salet'*

Salet A repeat-flowering Moss Rose with blooms of a good clear pink, and red moss. Unfortunately it is rather coarse both in flower and growth, although it is the most perpetual flowering in this class. Height 1.2m / 4ft. Bred by Lacharme (France) 1854.

Soupert et Notting A neat rose, which is rather different to other Mosses. The flowers are quite small, deep lilac-pink, neatly rounded and flat with closely packed petals, and have an attractive formality. The growth is short and bushy, to about 1m / 3ft, and it repeat flowers well in the late summer. Although the moss is not very conspicuous, this is a charming rose. Bred by Pernet Père (France) 1874.

William Lobb ('Old Velvet Moss') A tall and vigorous shrub of rather straggly growth, 1.8–2.5m / 6–8ft in height, with thorny stems and leaden-green foliage. The flowers are of the most beautiful colouring: a dark crimson-purple turning to lavender and eventually almost to grey, the reverse of the petals being light magenta. They are held in large, open sprays, have plentiful green moss and a strong fragrance. This is an ideal rose for the back of the border, where it will look over the top of other smaller shrubs without showing its rather ungainly growth. It may even, as Graham Thomas suggests, be allowed to scramble into other shrubs, often combining with them to make pleasing colour effects. It is a tough and fairly healthy rose, although it does sometimes succumb to powdery mildew. Raised by Laffay (France) 1855.

William Lobb is a tall and vigorous shrub. The flowers are dark crimson-purple turning to lavender and eventually almost to grey, held in large, open sprays

Part 2

THE REPEAT-FLOWERING
OLD ROSES

Towards the end of the eighteenth century something happened that was to change our garden roses for ever. As European travellers and traders began to throw just a little chink of light on the ancient mysteries of China, it was inevitable that plants of that massive land should be brought back to Europe. China is probably the finest source of plant material in the world, and is certainly the home of some of the most beautiful wild roses, having to its credit somewhere in the region of one hundred different species. Before Europeans had seen these in the wild, certain garden hybrids were brought to Britain. These were to be known as the China Roses. Although not particularly striking in appearance, they did have one very important characteristic: the ability to flower not just in early summer but throughout the growing season. They were, as we say, repeat flowering, perpetual flowering, remontant, or recurrent, according to which term you choose. It is interesting and rather surprising that China, in spite of her wealth of wild roses and the fact that she has a very long and honourable tradition of gardens and flowers, never rated the rose very highly. The Chinese were essentially gardeners and their interests centred around peonies, chrysanthemums and other flowers, but only to a small degree the rose, although we do from time to time find it depicted on old pottery and in pictures.

The repeat-flowering characteristic of the China Roses was not entirely new —as we have already seen the Autumn Damask Rose had the same ability which it owed to *Rosa moschata*, itself recurrent flowering from late summer onwards. The ability to flower repeatedly is a phenomenon which does not usually occur in nature and is the result of a sport or mutation in the mechanism of the plant. With one or two exceptions wild roses first of all send up tall non-flowering shoots, and it is only in the next season that the shorter flowering shoots appear on these. In the case of the China Rose, something went wrong—or perhaps I should say, for us, went right. A plant appeared which lost its ability to form its main non-flowering stems and produced only flowering stems, with the result that we had a bush on which every stem produced a flower. Having flowered, the rose would normally busy itself with the production of strong stems ready to bear next season's flowers and fruit, but in this case the plant continued to flower without thought for the future. This important fact was, no doubt, noted by some observant and long-forgotten Chinaman, who subsequently propagated the plant. Whoever he was, he made a most important contribution to our garden roses—greater perhaps than anyone has done since, for this discovery doubled or even trebled the period over which we can enjoy roses.

The China Rose originally arrived in the British Isles in four different varieties. These became known as 'Slater's Crimson China' (introduced 1792); 'Parsons' Pink China' (Old Blush China, brought to Europe 1751, introduced 1793); 'Hume's Blush China' (1809); and 'Parks' Yellow Tea-Scented China' (1824). The origin of these roses is difficult to trace. 'Parks' Yellow' can only have been the result of a cross between *R. gigantea*—which bears the largest flowers of all rose species—and a China Rose.

It may be thought that the arrival of these roses would have caused a great flurry of interest among plant breeders, but this was not the case. For one thing, the existing native roses were far more showy by comparison. Before long, however, hybrids with the European roses did appear, but the gene that provided the repeat-flowering characteristic was what is known as recessive, with the result that the first hybrids were once flowering. It was only when these hybrids were again crossed with the China Roses that perpetual-flowering varieties began to appear and the revolution began. From then on things moved apace and the rose has never looked quite the same again.

This revolution was not confined to the repeat-flowering characteristic. The China Rose, with its connection with *R. gigantea*, was an entirely different rose. Whereas the European roses tended to have rough-textured leaves and many thorns, the China Roses had smooth leaves and few thorns. Moreover, their whole character was different. This provided great opportunities but, as is so often the case, also certain dangers.

'Slater's Crimson China' brought the richer and purer reds we now find in many roses. Previously the crimsons invariably turned to purple and mauves, though often with very pleasing effect. 'Parks' Yellow' gave us the larger, thicker, more waxy petals of *R. gigantea*. It also provided the Tea Rose scent and tints of yellow, though not yet a rich yellow.

As China blood became mingled with that of the Gallicas and Damasks, a great variety of new roses appeared, most of them with the ability to flower repeatedly, if not well at least to some extent.

In this chapter we cover the various classes which, while showing signs of having a strong China influence, still bear flowers with much of the character of the truly Old Rose and can generally be described as shrubs rather than bushes. These include the Portland Roses, the Bourbons, the Hybrid Perpetuals and the Tea Roses, as well as the China Roses themselves, although there is some doubt as to the inclusion of China blood in the Portlands—at least in the early varieties. All these groups tend to have foliage nearer the China Roses than the European roses; they are, in fact, beginning to look more like the Modern Roses, but the flowers retain the full, open Old Rose formation.

*Given a warm sheltered position near a wall, the excellent **Mutabilis** will form a 2.5m/8ft shrub or climber which will flower as constantly as any other rose*

This second part of the Old Rose history is rather in the nature of an unfinished story. The flower formation and shrub-like growth of the Old Roses were soon to be superseded by the pointed buds and low bush growth of the Hybrid Teas before breeders had brought Old Roses to their full potential. It was unfortunate that the development of the two types was not allowed to continue side by side, but it was not to be. Nonetheless, we have here some roses of real value which it would be a great shame to lose. Happily, as things stand at the moment, there is very little likelihood of this happening.

China Roses

China Roses differ in character to most other garden roses, even to those unnumbered masses that are their heirs. They are altogether lighter in growth. This is perhaps because they are diploid, whereas the majority of garden roses are tetraploid; that is to say their cells contain two sets of chromosomes, whereas it is more usual to have four sets which result in larger cells and therefore heavier growth. China Roses have airy, twiggy growth and rather sparse foliage, with pointed leaves, like a lighter version of a Hybrid Tea. Both growth and leaves are often tinted with red when young. The flowers are not showy, nor are they particularly shapely, but they do have a certain unassuming charm. They have an exceptional ability to repeat their flowering, and are seldom without blooms throughout the summer. Their colours are unusual in that they intensify with age, rather than pale, as is the case with European roses.

Until recently the origins of the China Rose remained a mystery. We know of the four original varieties described in the introduction to this chapter, but the wild form eluded us. It would appear that this rose was found by Mr Mikinori Ogisu of Tokyo in the Chinese Province of Sichuan. A photograph of this rose appeared in the Royal National Rose Society's Journal, *The Rose*, in September 1986, together with an article by Graham Thomas. Mr Ogisu describes it as growing into trees to a height of up to 3m / 10ft, and bearing flowers of 5–6cm / 2–2½in wide, which vary in colour from pink to crimson — the colour being darker in regions of higher altitude. Previously this rose had been seen by Dr Augustine Henry in 1884, who described it in *The Gardener's Chronicle* in 1902, where it was illustrated with a drawing. The species is known as *R. chinensis* var. *spontanea*.

The China Roses of our gardens vary considerably according to the conditions under which they are grown. In an open position in the British Isles they will rarely reach much more than 60–90cm / 2–3ft in height, although in more favourable areas they will grow much taller. In countries with warmer climates they will make quite large shrubs of 1.8m / 6ft and more. As to position, it is best to select a sheltered corner of the garden, perhaps with the protection of a south-facing wall which is shielded from the wind. Here they will grow much nearer their full potential. Having said all this, China Roses are not really tender and can be relied on to withstand all but the very hardest winters in the British Isles.

The light growth and dainty flowers of China Roses make them particularly suitable for mixing with other plants, especially where something heavier and more robust might be out of place. They require fertile soil, or at least soil that has been well manured, but unlike other repeat-flowering Old Roses they dislike hard pruning, and this should usually be done only to maintain the shape of the shrub and to remove dead and ageing growth.

Bengal Crimson (*R.* × *odorata* 'Bengal Crimson', 'Sanguinea', 'Rose de Bengale') This rose is rarely seen and rarely available in the UK but well worth seeking out if you have a warm, sheltered spot. It much prefers warm climates where it has the advantage of flowering 12 months of the year. The flowers are truly single, about 9cm / 3½in across and of the purest blood red that fades to a more crimson shade as they age. There is a light tea fragrance. Interestingly, although not a true species, it comes true from seed. In the British Isles it will make a rounded bushy plant about 1– 1.2m / 3–4ft tall but will grow twice that height in hotter climates. Introduced *c.*1824.

Comtesse du Cayla A dainty little shrub of 90cm / 3ft in height with almost single flowers of varying shades of coppery-pink, eventually becoming salmon-pink with yellow tints at the base of the petal. The foliage is purplish-bronze when young. Tea Rose scent. Raised by P. Guillot (France) 1902.

Cramoisi Supérieur
has short, twiggy growth
and small, cupped,
crimson flowers produced
in small clusters

Cramoisi Supérieur Small, cupped, fragrant flowers of a clear unfading crimson, produced in small clusters. The growth is short and twiggy, about 90cm / 3ft in height in a warm situation. There is also a good climbing form, 'Cramoisi Supérieur Grimpante'. Bred and introduced by Coquereau, 1832.

Fabvier ('Madame Fabvier', 'Colonel Fabvier') A small low-growing plant of about 30cm / 1ft in height, rather similar in habit to a Polyantha Rose. The flowers are small and bright scarlet with a white streak in their petals. It is constantly in bloom and the petals fall before they fade, giving an effect of continuing brilliance. Laffay (France) 1832.

*Low-growing **Fabvier** is constantly in bloom and has petals that fall before they fade, giving an effect of continuing brilliance*

Hermosa This shows all the signs of being a China Rose hybrid. We do not know what the other parent was, but certainly it is an excellent little rose. It has something of the appearance of a Bourbon Rose, but is smaller in all its parts and more delicate in appearance. The growth is branching

and more sturdy than most China Roses, bearing small lilac-pink flowers of a pretty cupped formation. They are borne with admirable continuity throughout the summer. Slight fragrance. Bred and introduced by Marcheseau (France) 1834.

Hermosa, a China that has something of the appearance of a Bourbon Rose, is smaller in all its parts and more delicate in appearance

Le Vésuve ('Lemesle') Dainty scrolled buds of Tea Rose appearance, soft creamy-pink in colour, gradually deepening with age and finally taking on tints of carmine. The flowers have a Tea Rose fragrance and are produced continually on a branching twiggy bush which will, given a warm sheltered position, achieve 1.5m / 5ft in height, although 90cm / 3ft is more usual under average conditions. Introduced by Laffay (France) 1825.

Madame Laurette Messimy Long slender buds with only a few petals which open quickly. They are salmon-pink at first, shaded copper at the base of the petal, the open flower soon fading. It is the result of a cross between 'Rival de Paestum' and the Tea Rose 'Madame Falcot', and is, in fact, of somewhat Tea Rose appearance. It will grow to 1.2m / 4ft in height in a warm position. Bred by Guillot Fils (France) 1887.

Mutabilis ('Tipo Ideale') Often incorrectly known as *Rosa turkestanica*, this variety rivals the 'Old Blush China' for its excellence as a garden shrub. Its pointed copper-flame buds open to single copper-yellow flowers of butterfly daintiness, soon turning to pink and finally almost crimson. Given a warm sheltered position near a wall it will form a 2.5m / 8ft shrub which will probably flower as constantly as any other rose. In more exposed positions it is often quite small and frail in appearance. Apart from knowing that it comes from Italy in around 1900, we know little of the origins of this rose.

*Facing page, **Mutabilis** is a superb shrub especially in warmer areas, where it will flower continuously*

*The flowers of **Le Vésuve** have a Tea Rose fragrance and are produced continually on branched, twiggy growth*

*Old Blush China is
often the first rose to start
flowering in spring and the
last to finish in the winter*

Old Blush China ('Parsons' Pink China', *R.* × *odorata* 'Pallida') This is a very good garden shrub, with twiggy but quite robust growth and dainty flowers in small clusters. These are produced continually throughout the summer, starting early and finishing late, and for this reason it was formerly known as the Monthly Rose. The flowers are not large and have a loose informality. They are pale pink in colour, deepening with age. The bush usually grows to about 1.2m / 4ft in height but may be considerably taller in

favourable conditions. I have seen it growing as a 3m / 10ft shrub near to a wall in the warm climate of Pembrokeshire. It has a pleasing fragrance which has been described as being similar to that of a Sweet Pea. Introduced to England in 1789.

Rival de Paestum Long, pointed buds, tinted blush, opening to semi-double ivory-white flowers elegantly poised on a shrub some 1.2m / 4ft in height. Sometimes classified as a Tea Rose. Raised by Beluze 1841.

The long, pointed buds of **Rival de Paestum** *open to semi-double ivory-white flowers of poised elegance*

*Facing page, **Sophie's Perpetual** bears flowers of shapely cupped formation that are held in sprays against dark green foliage*

*The petals of **Viridiflora** have been replaced by numerous green sepals, giving it its other name - the Green Rose*

Sophie's Perpetual A beautiful rose found in an old garden, named by Humphrey Brooke and reintroduced in 1960. The flowers are quite small, of shapely cupped formation and held in small sprays. Their colour is a deep pink. Strong growth with few thorns and dark green foliage. The fragrance has been described as the closest to a perfume to be found in roses. It will grow into a 1.8m / 6ft shrub and may be used as a climber. Of obvious hybrid origin.

Viridiflora (the Green Rose) In this rose the petals are entirely missing and have been replaced by numerous green sepals giving the effect of a green rose. It is, no doubt, a sport from the 'Old Blush China', to which it is very similar in growth. It is of little value as a garden plant, except as a curiosity, although it may have its uses for inclusion in flower arrangements. Height 90cm / 3ft. Introduced 1855.

Portland Roses

The Portland Roses were the first family in which the China Rose played a part by passing on its ability to repeat flower. They had only a short period of popularity, for they were soon overtaken, first by the Bourbons, and not long after by the Hybrid Perpetuals – although in 1848 there were 84 varieties growing at Kew. Today only a handful remain, but they form, nonetheless, a not unimportant class, both for their beauty and as one of the parents of the Hybrid Perpetuals.

The origins of the Portland Roses are shrouded in mystery and writers tend to step lightly over the subject, but we do know that around the year 1800 the Duchess of Portland obtained from Italy a rose known as *Rosa paestana* or 'Scarlet Four Seasons' Rose', and that it was from this rose that the group developed. The Portland Rose was repeat flowering and was thought to have been the result of a cross between *Rosa gallica* var. *officinalis* and the repeat-flowering Autumn Damask, and certainly DNA analysis supports the presence of these two parents. Hurst seems to have had little to say on the subject, although he does note that Redouté's print of 1817 has the appearance of a China-Damask-French hybrid. I would thus assume Hurst had not seen the growing plant. One would expect there to be some China Rose influence (probably 'Slater's Crimson China'), although there is not much evidence of this in the plant. If this is so, it may well have inherited the recurrent-flowering characteristic from two different sources. The Portland Rose was sent from England to France where André Dupont, gardener to the Empress Josephine, named it 'Duchess of Portland', and it was not very long before the French had raised numerous varieties.

Portland Roses are not difficult to recognise. They usually show a strong Damask influence, but they are shorter in growth, perhaps 1.2m / 4ft in height. The flowers tend to have very little stem so that the leaves are packed closely around the flowers, forming what Graham Thomas describes as a rosette or shoulder of leaves.

Although they cannot be said to be graceful in growth, being rather upright, Portland Roses are well suited to smaller gardens as they form small, compact shrubs. Their virtue lies in the fact that, though repeat flowering, they retain much of the character of the truly Old Roses and have a strong Damask fragrance. Their ability to repeat is by no means unfailing and varies according to variety, but most of them can be relied on to provide flowers later in the year, many of them producing particularly beautiful Old Rose blooms.

Arthur de Sansal A compact, upright shrub with ample foliage, the attractive buds opening to form flat, neatly-shaped, very double dark crimson-purple flowers, paler on the reverse side of the petals. There is usually a button eye at the centre of the flower. Richly fragrant. Height 90cm / 3ft. Raised by Cochet (France) 1855.

Blanc de Vibert This variety bears prettily-cupped, many-petalled white flowers with a strong fragrance. It forms an upright bush with ample pale green Damask Rose foliage. Height 90cm / 3ft. Raised by Vibert (France), introduced 1847.

Arthur de Sansal
forms a compact, upright shrub with flat, very double dark crimson-purple flowers which are paler on the reverse

Comte de Chambord
*(and facing page) retains
the true Old Rose
character and repeat
flowers well, making it one
of the best and most
beautiful of all the
Portlands*

Comte de Chambord Very full quartered flowers of rich clear pink with a powerful Damask Rose fragrance. The growth is strong and rather upright, about 1.2m / 4ft in height, with ample foliage, the leaves coming all the way up to the flower in true Portland style. Here we have a rose that retains the true Old Rose character, while at the same time repeat flowering well. One of the best and most beautiful of this class. Raised by Moreau-Robert (France), introduced 1860.

Delambre A compact bush bearing full-petalled deep pink flowers against ample dark green foliage. Height 90cm / 3ft. Bred by Moreau-Robert (France) 1863.

Indigo The colour of this varies considerably according to climate and age of flower; it does include indigo although it may also be purple, crimson or deep mauve. The blooms and growth are typically Portland with fully double flowers and stiff stems. It repeat flowers and is relatively healthy. There is a delicious fragrance. Height 90cm / 3ft. Bred by Laffay (France) 1830.

Facing page, Portlands form a small but valuable group, their compact growth making them ideal for smaller gardens. Truly Old Rose in character, they have a strong fragrance and have the advantage of repeat flowering

***Indigo** flowers vary considerably in colour, creating a most attractive mixed effect*

Jacques Cartier ('Marchesa Boccella') Very similar to 'Comte de Chambord', but the shapely full-petalled flowers have, if anything, a little more refinement, although it is not such a good repeat flowerer. It has the same clear pink colouring, fading a little with age, and a button eye at the centre. The growth is compact and erect with light green Damask Rose foliage. Rich fragrance. Height 1.1m / 3½ft. Raised by Moreau-Robert (France), introduced 1868.

Marbrée Deep purple-pink flowers mottled with a paler pink and opening flat. The growth is strong and tall for a Portland, with plentiful dark green foliage. Slight fragrance. Height 1.2m / 4ft. Raised by Robert et Moreau (France) 1858.

Facing page, **Jacques Cartier** *has some of the most perfectly formed blooms of any variety*

Tall-growing **Marbrée** *has deep purple-pink flowers mottled with a paler pink which open flat*

Rose de Rescht, an excellent all-round variety, has beautiful blooms, a strong fragrance, good repeat flowering and attractive, healthy, rounded growth

Facing page, A worthy shrub for both summer and autumn, **Portland Rose** *has light crimson blooms with a strong Damask fragrance*

Portland Rose (the 'Scarlet Four Seasons' Rose', 'Duchess of Portland', 'Paestana', 'Portlandica') This forms an excellent bushy and rather spreading shrub of 90cm / 3ft in height with ample foliage. The flowers are semi-double opening wide and of light crimson colouring with conspicuous yellow stamens. A good garden shrub both in summer and autumn. Strong Damask fragrance.

Rose de Rescht A shapely, bushy shrub that has quite small neatly-formed very double flowers with closely-packed petals. The purplish-crimson blooms are nicely placed on short stems against ample rough-textured deep green foliage. There are signs of Gallica Rose influence both in flower and leaf, but the fact that it produces a second crop of flowers suggests its place is in this class. Delicious and strong fragrance. Height 90cm / 3ft. Brought to England by Miss Nancy Lindsay in the 1940s, possibly from Rasht on the Caspian Sea, Iran.

Rose du Roi,
a Portland, has had a
great influence on our
Modern Roses

Rose du Roi ('Lee's Crimson Perpetual') An interesting little rose which has had a great influence on our Modern Roses, being the channel through which we obtained the clear red colouring, first of all in the Hybrid Perpetuals, and from them in the Hybrid Teas of the present day. It is a short rather spreading bush and not particularly robust. The flowers are loosely double, crimson mottled with purple. Strong fragrance. It repeats well and is, all in all, a worthwhile rose in its own right. Raised by Lélieur (France), introduced by Souchet, 1815.

Rose du Roi à Fleurs Pourpres ('Roi des Pourpres', 'Mogador') Said to be a sport from 'Rose du Roi', its appearance casts some doubt on this. It is a pretty little rose with loosely formed purple flowers. Of spreading growth, it may achieve about 90cm / 3ft under suitable conditions. Introduced 1819.

Rose du Roi à Fleurs Pourpres bears flowers of a wonderful rich colour

Bourbon Roses

The origins of the Bourbon Rose make a fascinating story and illustrate very well how the various developments of the early roses always happened by chance, and sometimes in what seem to be the most unlikely places. These roses take their name from l'Île de Bourbon, a small island near Mauritius in the Indian Ocean, now known as Réunion. It is said that farmers of this island were in the habit of planting both the Autumn Damask and the 'Old Blush China' together as hedges. With so many of these roses growing in close proximity there was always a chance that a hybrid would arise, and this is what happened. The Parisian botanist Nicolas Bréon found a rose growing in the garden of a man named A. M. Perchern. This rose was intermediate between the Autumn Damask and the 'Old Blush China' and had been grown on the island for some years under the name 'Rose Edward'. Bréon sent seed of this rose to his friend Jacques, gardener to King Louis-Philippe, from which a rose called 'Rosier de l'Île de Bourbon' was raised. It was distributed in France in 1823 and two years later in England. Not much is known about the early development of these roses, for breeding was then still confined to the chance collection of seed, but we can be sure that several other roses played a part in their development.

The Bourbons represent the first real step towards the Modern Roses. Their flowers retain the character of the Old Roses with their strong fragrance, and they still have shrubby growth, but their leaves and stems begin to look more like those of the Hybrid Tea, and they are nearly all repeat flowering. Thus we have something of the best of both worlds. They are usually of robust growth and some highly desirable roses are to be found among them, although, in general, their resistance to blackspot is poor.

With Bourbons pruning becomes more important, particularly if we are to take advantage of their ability to flower a second time. Side shoots should be pruned back to three eyes, and strong main shoots reduced by one third. As the years go by, ageing and dead growth should also be removed. A liberal mulching with farmyard manure or compost, and an application of a rose fertilizer in spring (March in the UK) and again after the first crop of flowers will greatly improve the results. Immediate dead heading is also important.

Adam Messerich A late arrival on the scene. One of its parents was a Hybrid Tea, and this shows up in the rather modern appearance of its growth and foliage — it might be argued that it is not a Bourbon at all. However, this need not worry us as it is a good shrub which may also be grown as a climber or pillar rose. It is very vigorous, sending up long, slightly arching, almost thornless growth from the base of the plant. The flowers are large, semi-double, slightly cupped in shape and of a deep warm pink. The fragrance is strong, with a somewhat fruity, some say raspberry, flavour. It flowers freely in early summer but there are only occasional blooms later. Height 1.5m / 5ft. Bred by P. Lambert (Germany), introduced 1920.

Facing page, The blooms of **Adam Messerich** *have a strong fruity fragrance and are borne freely in early summer - though only occasionally later*

Boule de Neige A slender upright shrub of perhaps 1.5m / 5ft in height, its neat dark green foliage betraying its partly Tea Rose ancestry. The flowers are held in small clusters, and its small, round, crimson-tinted buds open to the most perfectly formed creamy-white blooms of posy freshness, the petals gradually turning back on themselves almost forming a ball. Add to this a strong fragrance and we have one of the most charming white Old Roses. Bourbon 'Blanche Lafitte' × the Tea Rose 'Sappho'. Bred by Lacharme (France) 1867.

Bourbon Queen ('Queen of the Bourbons', 'Reine des Îles Bourbon') A rose frequently found surviving in old gardens after many years. It may be grown either as a tall rather open shrub of up to 1.8m / 6ft in height, or as a climber; on a wall it can achieve 3–3.5m / 10–12ft. The flowers are cupped and rather loosely formed with exposed stamens and crinkled petals. They are medium pink veined with deeper pink paling towards the edges. Strong fragrance. Raised by Mauget (France), introduced 1834.

Facing page, **Boule de Neige** *has small crimson-tinted buds that open to perfectly formed blooms*

Bourbon Queen *may be grown either as a tall rather open shrub or as a climber*

One of three Bourbon roses with striped flowers, **Commandant Beaurepaire** *is notable for its lovely mixture of colours, which are at their best in cool weather*

Facing page, **Coupe d'Hébé** *has slightly quartered flowers of pale pink and tall, narrow growth that is perhaps rather too upright*

Commandant Beaurepaire ('Panachée d'Angers') The three Bourbon Roses with striped flowers—'Commandant Beaurepaire', 'Honorine de Brabant' and 'Variegata di Bologna'—are all rather similar. This one is notable for the lovely mixture of colours in its flowers: carmine pink flecked and striped with mauve, purple, scarlet and pale pink, and this so variously that they might be described in a dozen different ways. These colours are at their best in cool weather, as they tend to be rather muddy in very hot sun. The flowers are shallowly cupped in shape, strongly fragrant and produced very freely. This rose forms a dense leafy bush of strong growth that requires some thinning at pruning time to maintain the quality of its flowers. The height is 1.5m/5ft and as much across. It flowers only in early summer. Raised by Moreau-Robert (France) 1874.

Coupe d'Hébé Cupped flowers of pale pink opening full and slightly quartered. The growth is tall, narrow and rather too upright, with light green foliage. It may be grown as a Climber. Bred from a Bourbon hybrid × a China hybrid. Laffay (France) 1840.

Honorine de
Brabant *is one of three*
Bourbon Roses with
striped flowers

Facing page, **Louise**
Odier *is the most*
desirable of the recurrent-
flowering Old Roses

Honorine de Brabant A rose similar to 'Commandant Beaurepaire' but paler in colour — light pink splashed with shades of crimson and purple. It has the advantage over 'Commandant Beaurepaire' in that it repeat flowers quite well, the later flowers often being of better quality in the less intense sunlight of late summer. They are of shallow cupped shape, opening quartered, with a strong fragrance. The growth is robust and bushy, to about 1.8m / 6ft, with ample foliage. It may also be grown as a climber.

Louise Odier A rose out of very much the same mould as 'Reine Victoria', having all its virtues but with more robust and bushy growth. The flowers are beautifully formed, cupped at first, opening flatter and neatly rounded, with each petal precisely in place. Their colour is a lovely warm pink and they have a rich fragrance. Like 'Reine Victoria' it repeats well throughout the summer, and for me it is the most desirable of the recurrent-flowering Old Roses. Height 1.5m / 5ft. I have used this rose for breeding and the results suggest that it has some Noisette in its make up. Raised by Margottin (France), introduced 1851.

Madame Ernst Calvat is a sport of 'Madame Isaac Pereire' and is similar in every way, except for its medium pink colouring

Facing page, Madame Isaac Pereire is a vigorous shrub that will hold its own in a mixed border, here with a tall campanula and Sambucus nigra 'Marginata'

Madame Ernst Calvat A sport from 'Madame Isaac Pereire', described below. It is similar in every respect, except for the colour which is a medium pink. In my opinion the flowers are a little less happy in this colour than in the deeper shades of its parents, often appearing rather coarse, but as with so many roses we get the occasional perfect flower, particularly in autumn, that makes it all worth while. It has the same strong growth and rich fragrance as 'Madame Isaac Pereire'. Height 1.8m / 6ft. Discovered by Vve Schwartz (France) 1888.

Madame Isaac Pereire A vigorous shrub some 2m / 7ft in height with large, thick, deep green foliage. It bears huge flowers, perhaps 12cm / 5in across. These are cupped at first and quartered on opening, the petals being rolled back at the edges. The colour is a very deep pink shaded with magenta, giving a rich effect, and there is an extremely powerful fragrance. It flowers well in the autumn when it often produces some of its best blooms. A sumptuous beauty, especially when well grown. The parentage is not recorded. Bred by Garçon (France) 1881.

A most beautiful rose, **Madame Lauriol de Barny** *bears silky, fragrant quartered blooms of silvery pink*

Facing page, **Madame Pierre Oger** *is similar to 'Reine Victoria' in every respect except for the colour of the chaliced blooms*

Madame Lauriol de Barny A most beautiful rose carrying silky, richly fragrant quartered blooms of silvery pink colouring. They are held in weighty, slightly drooping sprays on a vigorous 1.8m/6ft shrub, which may also be trained as a climber. It has a good crop of flowers in early summer but there are rarely any blooms later. Raised by Trouillard (France) 1868.

Madame Pierre Oger A sport from 'Reine Victoria', to which it is similar in every respect except for the colour of the flowers. This is a pale creamy blush, giving the flowers a refinement exceeding even that of its parent, the beautiful chaliced blooms taking on the appearance of the most delicate porcelain. In very hot weather the colour tends to deepen and harden on the sunny side of the blooms, and in the rain the petals become speckled. The growth is narrow and upright, about 1.5m/5ft in height. Fragrant. Discovered by A. Oger (France) 1878.

*Sharing many traits with 'Madame Isaac Pereire', **Mrs Paul** has large blush-white flowers with a strong perfume*

Mrs Paul Probably a seedling from 'Madame Isaac Pereire' with which it shares many characteristics. It has large blush-white flowers with a strong perfume. The growth is robust though rather floppy and may require a little support. Plentiful large leaves. Height 1.5m/5ft. Bred by George Paul (England), introduced by Paul & Sons 1891.

Prince Charles Dark purple-crimson flowers turning almost lilac as they age. They are large, flat when open and have petals of a veined and crimpled appearance. The growth is strong, about 1.5m / 5ft in height, with large leaves and few thorns. It has little fragrance and is not recurrent. One of the few dark-coloured roses in this class. A sport or seedling of 'Bourbon Queen', introduced 1842.

With its dark purple-crimson flowers, **Prince Charles** *is one of the few dark-coloured Bourbons*

Reine Victoria In this rose and its sport, 'Madame Pierre Oger', we have two of the most beautiful and best loved roses of the late 19th century. They both form slender shrubs of about 1.5m / 5ft in height, with the blooms elegantly poised above the foliage, indicating a close relationship with China Roses. The flowers are medium sized, chalice shaped rather than cupped, the petals incurving towards the centre to provide a charming enclosed effect and holding their form to the end. The colour is lilac-pink on the outside and paler within. This variety has few rivals among the Old Roses in its ability to flower repeatedly throughout the summer. Unfortunately, as so often happens, along with this goes a greater tendency to blackspot. Fragrant. Height 1.2m / 4ft. Bred by J. Schwartz (France), introduced 1872.

Sir Joseph Paxton A vigorous, healthy and sturdy rose with very full cup-shaped flowers held in small clusters. The flowers are particularly strongly coloured and the petals have beautiful colour shadings; the base colour is bright rose-pink with crimson tints running through it. Unfortunately it doesn't repeat flower. There is a medium fragrance. Height 1.2m / 4ft by the same across. Bred by Laffay (France) 1852.

*Facing page, **Reine Victoria** has few rivals among the Old Roses in its ability to flower repeatedly throughout the summer*

*The flowers of **Sir Joseph Paxton** are very full cup shaped and are held in small clusters*

Souvenir de la
Malmaison *has
flowers of truly Old Rose
persuasion and foliage of
somewhat Modern
appearance, seen here in
the climbing form*

Souvenir de la Malmaison This rose was named in memory of the Empress Josephine's famous garden at Malmaison and is one of the most popular of the Bourbon Roses. It is available both as a bush and a climber, the bush being a short rather spreading shrub of about 90cm / 3ft in height. The flowers are a delicate blush-pink which pales a little with age. They are cup-shaped at first, later becoming flat and distinctly quartered to form a large and beautiful flower about 12cm / 5in across, with a fragrance similar to that of a Tea Rose. Raised in 1843 by J. Beluze of France, from a cross between the Bourbon Rose 'Madame Desprez' and a Tea Rose, it has, as we might expect, foliage of rather Modern appearance, although the flowers are of truly Old Rose persuasion. It is a reliable repeat flowerer. The growth is rather too short for the flowers, and it is, perhaps, better in its climbing form.

Souvenir de Saint Anne's An almost single sport of 'Souvenir de la Malmaison', found by Graham Thomas in Lady Ardilaun's garden at St Anne's, near Dublin. With extra generous treatment, it is capable of forming a fine shrub of 2m / 7ft in height. The large flowers are a delicate blush-pink colouring and have a nice clean-cut appearance. Rather surprisingly, unlike 'Souvenir de la Malmaison', it has a strong fragrance. Graham Thomas told me that this stems from *Rosa moschata* in its parentage, in which the fragrance comes from the stamens rather than the petals. Of course, this rose does have stamens, whereas its parent does not. Introduced 1950.

Variegata di Bologna The last of our trio of striped Bourbon Roses, and of more recent origin, having been bred in Italy by A. Bonfiglioli as late as 1909. The flowers are white, clearly striped with dark crimson-purple, giving them a purity and freshness that is very appealing, particularly in cool weather. They are fully double, cupped in shape, globular at first and quartered when open, and have a strong perfume. This rose has ample foliage and forms a dense shrub of 1.5–1.8m / 5–6ft or will climb to 3m / 10ft. A distinct and beautiful rose but susceptible to blackspot.

***Variegata di Bologna**, arguably the most attractive of the striped Old Roses, has flowers of a wonderful freshness and purity*

Tea Roses

The Tea Roses were the result of crossing two of the original China Roses, 'Hume's Blush China' (*Rosa × odorata* 'Odorata') and 'Parks' Yellow Tea-Scented China' (*Rosa × odorata* 'Ochroleuca') with various Bourbon and Noisette Roses. The first Tea Rose was introduced in 1835 and most appropriately named 'Adam', having been bred by an English nurseryman of that name. The class was originally known as Tea Scented China Roses, but this was soon abbreviated to Tea Roses. How they came to be known by this name is a mystery; there is, in fact, a range of fragrances to be found amongst them, but none of them, to my nose at least, has much in common with that of tea, although Graham Thomas insists that the scent of a typical Tea Rose is exactly like that of a freshly opened packet of China tea. However this may be, we still refer to certain roses as having a Tea Rose scent, and the name has now acquired a meaning of its own.

The Tea Rose was destined to become one of the parents of the Hybrid Tea, and could perhaps be best described as a rather slender version of that class while at the same time exhibiting a fairly close affinity to the twiggy, branching growth of the China Rose. Like the Chinas they are diploids. The popular, rather romanticised impression of a Tea Rose is of a long, slender and refined bud of the most delicate colouring, but this is only partly true; in fact they come in various forms and sometimes in quite harsh colours.

These roses cannot be recommended for general garden use in the UK; indeed I am not entirely sure that I would include them in this book were it not for the fact that they complete the historical picture. I have grown a number of them in my garden but have never found them satisfactory in our climate. If they survive the winter they are frequently cut back by frost and, although some are hardier than others, they often have the appearance of rather run-down Hybrid Teas. When grown in the warmer parts of the British Isles, such as Cornwall or Devon, it might be quite a different matter, and I have seen them growing as fine large shrubs in Mediterranean countries. If space can be found for them in a cold greenhouse, you may expect some very beautiful roses and the connoisseur may feel this worthwhile; after all, is it not true that many alpine plant enthusiasts go to equal lengths to grow their own particular treasures? Another less extreme method is to plant them against a warm and sheltered wall and treat them as short climbers.

However, it is very worthwhile planting Tea Roses in countries with warm and frost-free climates — most of the survivors in this class have come from such regions. The climbing Teas are usually much hardier and can be recommended for the average garden. Whether this is due to different breeding or to the fact that they are usually grown on walls, I cannot say — perhaps it is a bit of both.

Tea Roses prefer a well-drained, fertile soil and, as the reader will have gathered, should be planted in a warm and sheltered position. Like their

parents the China Roses, they object to too much pruning. This should consist only of the thinning out of old growth, the removal of dead wood, and general maintenance of the shape of the bush. Height will vary enormously according to climate. They seldom achieve more than 90cm / 3ft in the United Kingdom, but I have no doubt that in more southerly countries they could form much larger bushes.

Included here is a short list of Tea Roses that are still obtainable and mainly those with flowers in softer shades as I think these are more appealing. As I have not grown many of them under garden conditions, I have not had sufficient experience of some of the varieties to say which are the best.

Archiduc Joseph One of the hardiest of the Tea Roses, forming a strong bush or climber, with plentiful dark green foliage. The flowers are of a purplish-pink, opening flat with many petals, gradually turning to blush at the centre. Height 1.5m / 5ft. A seedling from 'Madame Lombard'. Bred by Nabonnand (France) 1892.

Catherine Mermet Once widely grown for the cut-flower trade. When well grown it has exquisitely formed buds, blush-pink at the centre and tinted lilac-pink at the edges. Only suitable for the greenhouse in the UK. Height 1.2m / 4ft. Bred by Guillot Fils (France) 1869.

Catherine Mermet
has exquisitely formed
buds and was once widely
grown for the cut-flower
trade

Dr. Grill (Docteur Grill) Pointed rose-pink buds shaded with copper, opening flat and full petalled. Branching growth. Fragrant. Height 90cm / 3ft. 'Ophirie' × 'Souvenir de Victor Hugo'. Bred by Bonnaire (France) 1886.

Homère Nicely cupped soft pink flowers with red tints at the edges, paling almost to white at the centre. An early variety that is hardier than most. It has bushy, twiggy growth with dark green foliage. Height 90cm / 3ft. Bred by Robert et Moreau (France) 1858.

Lady Hillingdon The only bush Tea Rose that can be said to be in anything like general circulation, and virtually as hardy as a Hybrid Tea. The recorded parentage is 'Papa Gontier' × 'Madame Hoste', both of which are Tea Roses, but this is doubtful due to the fact that the chromosome count indicates a cross with a Hybrid Tea. This illustrates very well that we should not place too much credence on early breeding records. 'Lady Hillingdon' has large petals, forming long slender buds of a lovely deep apricot-yellow which eventually open to rather shapeless flowers with a strong Tea Rose fragrance. It has fine contrasting dark green foliage which is coppery-mahogany when young. There is a particularly good climbing sport, better by far than the bush, and it is wiser to grow this form where space is available. Height 1.2m / 4ft. Bred by Lowe & Shawyer (UK) 1910.

Maman Cochet,
with its pale pink globular blooms featuring lemon-yellow shades at the base, was once a famous exhibition rose

Madame Bravy ('Adele Pradel', 'Madame de Sertat') Large creamy-white flowers shaded buff, with a strong Tea Rose fragrance. Height 90cm / 3ft. Guillot Père (France) 1846.

Maman Cochet Large globular blooms of pale pink, deepening towards the centre with lemon-yellow shades at the base. The growth is quite vigorous with dark green foliage. Once a famous exhibition rose. Height 90cm / 3ft. 'Marie van Houtte' × 'Mme Lombard'. Bred by Cochet (France) 1893.

Marie van Houtte Large pointed buds of cream tinged carmine-pink, with buff at the base of the petals. Fragrant. Sprawling habit. Height 90cm / 3ft. 'Madame de Tartas' × 'Madame Falcot'. Ducher (France) 1871.

Papa Gontier Long, pointed, deep pink buds, with the reverse side of the petals carmine-red, opening semi-double. Bushy growth. Height 90cm / 3ft. Nabonnand (France) 1883.

*Fragrant **Marie van Houtte** has large pointed buds and a sprawling habit*

Triomphe de Luxembourg has salmon-pink full-petalled flowers borne in clusters

Perle des Jardins Pointed buds developing into fragrant full-petalled flowers of a straw-yellow colour. These fail to open well in damp weather. The growth is slender but reasonably hardy. Fragrant. Height 90cm / 3ft. 'Madame Falcot' × a seedling. Levet (France) 1874.

Triomphe de Luxembourg Full-petalled flowers borne in clusters. Salmon-pink becoming salmon-buff. Height 90cm / 3ft. Hardy (France) 1839.

Hybrid Perpetual Roses

We now reach the final stage of development of the rose before arriving at the Hybrid Teas which are, of course, the predominant roses of the present day. None of the classes described so far can be said to be in any way pure or clearly defined in so far as their origins are concerned, although they may be quite distinct in their general character and appearance. When we come to the Hybrid Perpetuals this is more than ever true. They can best be described as an idea rather than as roses of any definite origins. They are, in fact, an amalgamation of various roses with certain objectives in view—for it is at this stage that large-scale breeding comes into its own—with breeders raising numerous seedlings in the hope of arriving at an ideal. William Paul tells us that the French breeder Laffay raised up to 200,000 seedlings annually—more than many large-scale breeders grow today.

It cannot be said that breeding on such a scale led to an all round improvement; indeed there is, to me, a decline in the beauty of the rose since Hybrid Perpetuals first appeared. It is true that, as their name suggests, the Hybrid Perpetuals are repeat flowering, but they are rather clumsy and their growth too tall, narrow and upright to be suitable for use as shrubs in the garden. The nature of their development was in no small degree due to the advent of the rose show which was, during the latter half of the 19th century, at the height of its popularity. Roses were exhibited in boxes in which six or more blooms would be placed at equal distances in order to show each of them individually. So keen was the competition that it resulted in a tendency to breed for exhibition only, and the flower as a bud became the exhibitor's ideal. Unfortunately this led to the notion of a rose perfect in bud formation only, while the open bloom, so much appreciated by Old Rose enthusiasts today, was given little regard. At the same time, and equally unfortunately, the breeders' attention was centred on the flower and habit of growth was ignored, often resulting in tall ungainly plants and poor resistance to disease. As garden plants they left much to be desired.

There are, however, some beautiful Hybrid Perpetuals still surviving, particularly those of earlier date, and many of them are well worth a place in the garden. It is these I include here. A few may be a little ungainly, but they are beautiful as cut flowers and do have at least three virtues: they are nearly all very fragrant, they are recurrent flowering, and many have the Old Rose flower formation. In this class we also find varieties of a rich pure crimson colouring, something rarely found in roses before the latter half of the 19th century.

Hybrid Perpetuals are gross feeders and repay generous treatment. Some, if left to their own devices, become too tall, and it is best to prune them down by about half their height to maintain reasonable proportions and ensure quality and continuity of bloom.

Arrillaga A very late arrival with interesting parentage (*Rosa centifolia* × 'Mrs John Laing') × 'Frau Karl Druschki', and therefore by no means a pure Hybrid Perpetual, if indeed there is such a thing. It forms a tall shrub, often growing to a height of over 1.8m/6ft. The flowers are in the Old Rose tradition, soft pink in colour, with a light fragrance. The first flowering is very prolific, but there is only an occasional bloom later in the summer. Bred by Schoener (USA), introduced 1929.

Baroness Rothschild produces some of the most beautiful flowers among the Hybrid Perpetuals - large, shallowly cupped, and often of the most perfect formation

Baroness Rothschild Large shallowly cupped flowers, frequently of the most perfect formation, the petals later recurving. They are of a soft pink colour, deepening towards the centre. The growth is erect, to 1.2m / 4ft, and thorny, with greyish-green foliage coming close up to the flower in the manner of a Portland Rose — to which it is probably closely related. It is free flowering and repeats quite well. This variety produces some of the most beautiful flowers in this section — it is unfortunate that it has little fragrance. A sport of 'Souvenir de la Reine d'Angleterre'. Discovered by Pernet Père (France) 1868.

Baron Girod de l'Ain A 'Eugène Fürst' sport, discovered by Reverchon of France in 1897. Unlike many Hybrid Perpetuals it forms a broad shapely shrub which grows strongly without being too upright. It has fine large foliage although disease resistance is poor. The flowers, like those of its parent, are a dark heavy crimson, but with the added and unusual attraction that the petals are neatly edged with a thin line of white. They are large and of shapely cupped formation, and their colour holds well, showing off the dual effect to perfection. It repeats quite well under good conditions and has a rich fragrance. Height 1.2m / 4ft.

*A sport of 'Eugène Fürst', **Baron Girod de L'Ain** has flowers of a dark heavy crimson neatly edged with white*

Baronne Prévost Large flowers in the Old Rose tradition, opening flat and quartered with a small button eye. The colour is pale rose-pink. Its growth is strong and very upright, about 1.2m/4ft in height. Fragrant. Bred by M. Desprez (France) 1841.

Comtesse Cécile de Chabrillant The Hybrid Perpetuals are not particularly known for their well formed blooms but Comtesse Cécile has most attractive, neat, rounded flowers. The overall colour is a rich pink but close examination reveals veining in many other shades of pink and a much paler pink on the reverse. It makes an attractive, reasonably compact shrub that flowers freely and, if dead headed, repeats well too. Like most in this group it can be grown as a short climber if lightly pruned. Strongly fragrant. A beautiful rose that should be more widely planted. Height and spread 1.2m/4ft. Bred by Marest (France) 1858.

*Facing page, **Baronne Prévost** has magnificent, perfectly formed blooms and strong upright growth*

***Comtesse Cécile de Chabrillant** is a beautiful Hybrid Perpetual with neat, rounded flowers deserving of being grown more widely*

Duke of Edinburgh *is one of the best of the bright red Hybrid Perpetuals, with full and fragrant blooms*

Facing page, ***Empereur du Maroc*** *requires a high standard of cultivation and is notable for its dark, velvety maroon-crimson colouring*

Duke of Edinburgh One of the best of the bright red Hybrid Perpetuals, forming a strong erect bush of about 90cm / 3ft in height. The flowers are full, of open incurved formation and fragrant, repeating quite well in the autumn. A hybrid of 'Général Jacqueminot'. Bred by George Paul (England) 1868.

Empereur du Maroc This variety is chiefly notable for the richness of its dark velvety maroon-crimson colouring. The flowers are not very large, opening flat, quartered, and well filled with petals which later reflex. Strong fragrance. Unfortunately the growth is rather weak, often resulting in poor flowers, and it requires a high standard of cultivation to produce worthwhile results. Its foliage is similar to that of a Hybrid Tea and is rather sparse. Only slightly recurrent. Height 90cm / 3ft. A seedling from 'Géant des Batailles'. Bred by Guinoisseau (France) 1858.

Ferdinand Pichard A striped rose that can be compared to the striped Bourbon varieties such as 'Commandant Beaurepaire'. Its flowers are pink, striped and splashed with crimson, the pink gradually fading almost to white while the crimson intensifies. They are of medium size, cupped in shape, not very full and fragrant. This rose forms a bushy shrub by the standards of a Hybrid Perpetual and flowers intermittently in late summer after the first crop. One of the best striped roses, as good as its Bourbon rivals, and perhaps the most suitable one for the smaller garden. Height 1.5m / 5ft. It was raised by R. Tanne of France as recently as 1921, and may well be a sport, but from which rose we do not know.

Fisher Holmes Pointed buds of scarlet and crimson, in the manner of a Hybrid Tea, the colour soon fading. It flowers both in summer and autumn and forms a healthy bush of about 1.2m / 4ft in height. Fragrant. Thought to be a seedling of 'Maurice Bernardin'. Bred by Verdier (France) 1865.

*Flowering both summer and autumn, **Fisher Holmes** bears pointed buds of scarlet and crimson*

*Facing page, **Ferdinand Pichard** is one of the best striped roses, as good as its Bourbon rivals, and the one to choose for the smaller garden*

Frau Karl Druschki *is a particularly tough and vigorous variety, although the flowers are very much like those of a Hybrid Tea*

Frau Karl Druschki ('Snow Queen', 'Reine des Neiges', 'White American Beauty') This rose belongs theoretically to the Hybrid Teas, being a cross between the Hybrid Perpetual 'Merveille de Lyon' and the Hybrid Tea 'Madame Caroline Testout', but the growth is so tall, up to 1.8m / 6ft in height, that it would be misleading to place it anywhere but here. The flowers, however, which are white with just a hint of lemon, are very close to those of a Hybrid Tea, and even today it is difficult to find a white Hybrid Tea flower that is better than this. It should be pruned as described in the introduction to this section, and will then form a tall, narrow, but slightly arching shrub, ideal for the back of the border. A group of two or three plants will knit together into a more shapely whole and give a more satisfactory effect. The foliage is light green. This is a tough old campaigner, although it may require spraying against mildew. Little or no fragrance. Raised by Lambert (Germany) 1901.

Général Jacqueminot ('General Jack', 'Jack Rose') An important variety in the development of the Modern Rose and perhaps of more interest for this than for any particular qualities of its own. In fact, most of the red roses of the present day relate back to this variety. It has rich crimson full-petalled flowers, opening rather untidily. The fragrance is particularly strong, and it was perhaps because of this rose and other similar Hybrid Perpetuals that the idea grew up that a red rose should have a strong rich fragrance — something that is sadly no longer always true today. Height 1.2m / 4ft. A hybrid between 'Gloire des Rosomanes' and 'Géant des Batailles'. Bred by Roussel (France) 1852.

Georg Arends ('Fortuné Besson') The breeding of this rose was 'Frau Karl Druschki' × 'La France' and it should, therefore, technically be placed with the Hybrid Teas. In practice it conforms to neither the Hybrid Teas nor the Hybrid Perpetuals, forming as it does a fine shapely, slightly arching shrub of 1.5m / 5ft in height with plentiful foliage. The flowers, on the other hand, are of distinctly Hybrid Tea persuasion, with large high-centered buds, the petals rolling back at the edges in the most attractive manner. Its colour is a clear rose-pink and it has a delicious fragrance. It is interesting to note that even a Hybrid Tea flower can be displayed to greater advantage on taller more shrubby growth. Raised by W. Hinner (Germany) 1910.

__Georg Arends__ bears blooms that have more in common with the typical Hybrid Tea, although they are produced on an attractively shaped shrub

Gloire de Ducher No other Hybrid Perpetual can match this variety for the splendour and richness of its flowers. They form very large informal cups of a deep purple-crimson shaded with maroon and are very fragrant. The blooms are particularly fine in the cool of the autumn. The growth is strong and rather sprawly, up to 2m/7ft in height, with large dark green leaves, and it might well be grown on a pillar or some other form of support. Its only drawback is a susceptibility to mildew. The parentage is not known. Bred by Ducher (France), introduced 1865.

Henry Nevard The most recent variety on my list, this rose was bred by Cant's of Colchester as late as 1924 and may have some Hybrid Tea in its make up. Its large deep crimson flowers are of cupped formation, with a powerful fragrance. They are held on long stems and repeat well. It has the tall upright habit of growth of a Hybrid Perpetual, perhaps 1.5m/5ft in height. The leaves are large, leathery and deep green.

*The powerfully fragrant **Henry Nevard** repeat flowers well and bears large deep crimson blooms of a cupped formation*

*Facing page, **Gloire de Ducher** is unmatched among the Hybrid Perpetuals for the splendour and richness of its flowers, which are particularly fine in the cool of the autumn*

Hugh Dickson Introduced in 1905, this was one of the most popular roses of its day, but in spite of this it does not have very much to recommend it—perhaps an indication of a decline in taste at the time, at least in so far as the rose was concerned. The flowers are large, scarlet-crimson, of a globular formation and produced on long shoots. They tend to lack character, being unshapely and rather coarse. The growth is very tall and ungainly, 2m/7ft, and it is perhaps more effective as a climber when it will easily achieve 3m/10ft. In its heyday it was frequently grown by pegging the long growth to the soil, so that it became effectively a climbing rose trailing along the ground. In this way numerous flower shoots are sent up along the stems, thus rendering it more suitable for bedding and providing an attractive 'Edwardian' effect. It flowers freely and recurrently and has a strong fragrance. The result of a cross between 'Lord Bacon' and 'Gruss an Teplitz', it was bred by H. Dickson (UK).

John Hopper Large, fragrant, lilac-pink flowers, deepening towards the centre. Vigorous, upright growth of 1.2m/4ft. 'Jules Margottin' × 'Madame Vidot'. Bred by Ward (UK) 1862.

Mabel Morrison A white sport of 'Baroness Rothschild', with the same Portland Rose characteristics and fine, shapely, shallowly cupped blooms. In autumn these will sometimes take on delicate blush tints. Very little scent. Discovered by Broughton (UK), introduced 1878.

John Hopper *has vigorous, upright growth and large, fragrant, lilac-pink flowers*

The white blooms of ***Mabel Morrison*** *sometimes take on delicate blush tints in the autumn*

Mrs John Laing is a good reliable rose, strongly scented and truly recurrent-flowering

Mrs John Laing Bred by Henry Bennett (UK), this may be regarded as his finest production. The flowers are large, deeply cupped, fully double and of a silvery-pink colouring. The growth is vigorous and upright, up to 1.2m / 4ft in height, with greyish-green foliage. 'Mrs John Laing' is a good reliable rose, truly recurrent flowering and strongly scented. Introduced in 1887, and one of the most popular roses of its time, it was said that Bennett received $45,000 for the distribution rights in America, an unheard of sum in those days. It was a seedling from 'François Michelon'.

Paul Neyron In the past this rose was regarded as having the largest flowers of all roses, and I suspect this may not be far from true today. It is in every way a large shrub, with large leaves and strong upright growth. Unfortunately with size comes clumsiness, as is so often the case, but if the flowers are cut and mixed with an arrangement of other flowers they can be very effective. Their colour is deep rose-pink flushed with lilac; they are cupped in shape and have a light fragrance. A cross between 'Victor Verdier' and 'Anna de Diesbach'. Bred and introduced by A. Levet (France) 1869.

Paul Neyron is in every way a large shrub, the flowers being some of the largest in the rose world

With its rich, velvety, crimson-maroon flowers, **Prince Camille de Rohan** *has the reputation of being the darkest of all roses*

Prince Camille de Rohan ('La Rosière') This variety has long held the reputation of being the darkest of all roses, and for this reason it continues to be in demand. I often fear that our customers may sometimes be disappointed, as it is of very weak growth, except when well grown under favourable conditions. It will form a bushy plant of 90cm / 3ft, bearing medium-sized, very double flowers of the richest velvety crimson-maroon. These are carried on weak stems but have a powerful fragrance. Raised by R. Verdier (France) 1861.

Reine des Violettes ('Queen of the Violets') A unique and charming rose with flowers closer to the Gallica Rose than to a typical Hybrid Perpetual. These are of full-petalled rosette formation, opening flat and quartered, with a button eye at the centre. Their colour is a deep velvet purple, turning with time to soft Parma-violet. The growth is upright, about 1.2–1.5m / 4–5ft in height, with grey-green foliage and hardly any thorns. It is reliably repeat flowering which, combined with the Old Rose form of flower, makes it particularly valuable. This rose requires good cultivation if it is to give of its best. A seedling from 'Pius IX'. Bred by Millet-Malet (France), introduced 1860.

Reine des Violettes is a beautiful rose that is closer to the Gallicas in appearance and very different from a typical Hybrid Perpetual

Roger Lambelin
bears deep crimson flowers whose petals are prettily edged with white but can prove a challenge to grow successfully

Roger Lambelin A sport from 'Prince Camille de Rohan', with all the failings of that rose, having very weak growth and poor flowers in all but the best of conditions. In appearance, too, it is similar to 'Prince Camille de Rohan', except that its deep crimson petals are prettily edged with white. Like its parent it can be beautiful if well grown, but for most gardens it might be better to grow 'Baron Girod de l'Ain', which is much stronger. Very fragrant. Height 90cm / 3ft. Discovered by Schwartz (France), distributed 1890.

Souvenir du Docteur Jamain Not a typical Hybrid Perpetual, this rose is notable for its deep, rich, dark crimson colouring and its equally deep and rich perfume. The flowers are of medium size, shallow, showing just a hint of their yellow stamens. It is repeat flowering but, like so many crimson roses, does not make ideal growth, being rather lean and lanky, and about 1.5–1.8m / 5–6ft in height. However, since there are few shrub roses with flowers of such colouring, it is worth its place in the garden. It has for some years also been on sale under the name of 'Souvenir d' Alphonse Lavallée', though it is impossible to see any difference between the two roses. Introduced by Lacharme (France) 1865.

Souvenir du Docteur Jamain is notable for its dark colouring and rich perfume

Facing page, **Vick's Caprice** *is very fragrant, recurrent flowering, with ample foliage that comes all the way up to the flower*

Ulrich Brünner
creates a spectacular display at Sissinghurst Castle in Kent, where its long shoots are pegged down

Triomphe de l'Exposition Full-petalled cherry-red flowers, opening almost flat and quartered, with a button eye. The growth is strong and bushy with recurrent blooms. Height 1.5m / 5ft. Bred and introduced by Margottin (France) 1855.

Ulrich Brünner A tall, robust and durable shrub of narrow, ungainly and upright habit, about 1.8m / 6ft in height. The flowers are cupped in form and of a rather crude pale crimson colour. Fine blooms are sometimes produced and it is a useful rose for cutting. Strong fragrance, recurrent flowering. It creates a spectacular display at Sissinghurst Castle in Kent, where its long shoots are pegged down. Bred by Levet (France) 1881.

Vick's Caprice Very large full-cupped flowers, their colouring of deep pink lightly striped with paler pink and white providing a delicate effect. It is very fragrant, recurrent flowering, with ample foliage that comes all the way up to the flower. Height 1.2m / 4ft. A sport from the pure pink 'Archiduchesse Élisabeth d'Autriche' (to which it frequently reverts) found in the garden of a Mr Vick of Rochester, New York, introduced 1891.

Old Roses Cultivation

Growing Old Roses is not difficult and much can be achieved simply by applying some basic common sense and giving them the minimum of attention. In fact if you do little more than working the soil to an acceptable tilth before planting your roses and firming them in gently, you can be sure of reasonable results. If you then prune your roses annually to a height of about two-thirds, you will have good results for years to follow - although this depends, to some degree, on the soil being of at least average quality.

However, it is true that you get out what you put in, and if you are prepared to expend a little more effort on your roses, this will not only give you a better display but also a great deal more satisfaction. The following notes are intended for those who wish to apply a little extra skill, care and knowledge to make the most of their roses. Before I go further, I should say that my advice is for gardeners in the British Isles and other temperate regions in the northern hemisphere. Gardeners in other climates will need to consult books on rose growing in their area.

Most ancestors of the garden rose are natives of more fertile areas of the world and it is worth giving them the best possible position - although non repeat-flowering Old Roses will usually withstand poorer conditions than the repeat-flowering Old Roses. (This is because the repeat-flowering roses have a much more strenuous task in providing continuous flushes of bloom.) Roses will not thrive if there is too much shade, so avoid any areas with overhanging trees. South-facing sites are entirely satisfactory; west-facing is no problem; east-facing sites are not quite so good; and a north-facing site is not really suitable at all.

The problem is not only a question of shade however; roses do not like competition from the roots of trees and shrubs, so it is better to plant well away from these. Neither do they like waterlogged soil. Then there is the question of rose re-plant disease, which occurs when a rose is planted in soil where roses have been grown before. In this situation they seldom thrive, even when the removed roses had been flourishing. The simple answer is instead to plant in a fresh site, or if this is not possible either to replace the soil with high quality new soil from a different site, or to treat the soil with ample quantities of humus and mycorrhizal fungi.

Preparing the Soil

Most roses are happiest in a heavier, humus-rich soil where they will grow larger and more strongly than in other soils, especially sandy ones. However, usually the gardener does not have much choice as regards soil type - although action can be taken to improve growing conditions. Light soils and medium loams will benefit from the addition of some humus, and chalky soils will need quite large quantities added since roses do not like too much lime. Likewise soils that are very heavy, such as a heavy clay, can be improved by adding liberal quantities of humus and grit.

It is advisable to prepare the soil thoroughly before you plant by incorporating humus to a depth of about 50cm/20 in. Remove the top soil and break up the sub-soil with a fork mixing in some humus, making sure it is well rotted. Mix in more of the same into the top soil and you are ready to plant. Alternatively, you may find it convenient to buy proprietary planting compost from your garden centre.

Planting

Planting of bare-rooted roses can be done at any time from autumn to late spring (early November to the end of April in the UK). If you purchase container-grown roses, these can be planted at any time of year. In my opinion, bare-rooted roses are marginally superior to those grown in pots but in any case, after a year or two, there is likely to be very little difference.

Planting should be at such a depth that the joint at which the rose has been budded onto the root stock lies just below the surface of the soil.

Pruning

People are often baffled by the whole question of pruning. This is usually because they think it is more difficult than it really is. I believe it is as much an art as a craft since a lot depends on the end you wish to achieve. Pruning may also depend, to some degree, on whether you require large individual flowers or a mass of smaller flowers. If you require the former, you will take away more wood; if you require the latter, you will leave more growth. Therefore the following instructions on pruning should not be taken too literally.

In the UK and elsewhere with relatively mild winters, pruning may be carried out at any time between the beginning of December and the end of February. Later pruning avoids any chance of the new shoots being caught by a late frost. I prefer earlier pruning for repeat-flowering roses, as they then get an earlier start, ensuring a longer season of flowering. It is always disappointing to see the last flush of bloom cut off by an early frost, but I would rather take this risk. In regions with cold winters, I would suggest it is better to delay pruning until spring growth is just starting.

On the whole, Old Roses require minimal pruning. When you receive your plants from your nurseryman, they will probably have been cut back sufficiently for the first year. If not, cut them down to about half their height. Very little pruning will be required in the first winter after planting. After that you should cut back any long main shoots by about one third of their length. The side shoots should be shortened to about 8cm/3in. In future, as the plant continues to mature, some of the growth will age and become unproductive - and other branches will die. These should be cut hard back to encourage new growth. Dead shoots must, of course, be removed completely.

Repeat-flowering Old Roses should receive very much the same treatment as those that only flower once although can be pruned harder if necessary. Many of the Bourbons and Hybrid Perpetuals will make tall and perhaps rather upright shrubs and in such cases it may suit your requirements to prune down to half their size.

Removing Suckers

Most roses are grown on root stocks and from time to time these may send up their own shoots which are generally known as 'suckers'. It is vital that these should be removed as soon as possible; otherwise they will soon take over the whole plant. Cut them as hard back as you can, digging down into the ground if necessary. It is advisable to take a little bark of the stock as you do this, thus eliminating all possibilities of it shooting again from the same point.

Maintenance

Having completed the pruning of our roses, it is now necessary to consider the question of maintenance. By pruning time the soil will have become rather compacted and a light pricking over of the soil with a fork to a depth of 5cm/2in will help to aerate it. It also gives a chance to remove any weeds that may have appeared. At this time it will be desirable to give the soil a feed in the form of a long-term fertilizer.

This done, it is a good idea to lay down a mulch of rotted garden compost, farmyard manure or green waste. This is not essential, but there is nothing better you can do in order to provide a good show of blooms in the coming summer. It will keep the soil cool and retain moisture - and at the same time help the life in the soil and provide an additional (although in practice small) source of nutrition. During the flowering season further dressings of fertilizers can be given at intervals. These should be relatively high in nitrogen and should be applied towards the end of a flush of bloom in order to encourage further growth and flowers for the next flush.

During the summer, dead-heading will be necessary for repeat flowering roses. This will stop the formation of hips, which use up the energy of the plant, thus inhibiting further bloom. This also gives us the opportunity to tidy up the shrub generally. If a rose does not repeat flower it may well produce decorative hips and so should not be dead headed.

Watering

Watering is not usually essential in the British climate, but there can be no doubt that it will ensure much better flowering and continuity of flowering. Most garden plants flower only once in a season, but those roses that have been bred to flower throughout the summer and into the autumn can only do this well if provided with moisture.

Diseases and Pests

Disease in roses is perhaps their greatest drawback as a garden plant, yet I do not think it is as bad as some people think. It is possible to grow roses without spraying, especially if they are scattered around the garden rather than planted close to each other in a rose garden. If you have a rose border or a rose garden it is almost always necessary to spray, although it does very much depend on your choice of varieties and how well they are looked after.

There are a number of excellent sprays on the market and they can be obtained from any garden centre. They should be used in accordance with the makers' instructions. Spraying should be done as soon as the disease appears (although taking care that there is no frost forecast) and repeated at intervals throughout the summer. The application of foliar feeds can also be most effective, especially those that contain seaweed.

There are four main diseases of roses:
Powdery Mildew This looks rather like a white powder. It is encouraged by dryness at the roots and so can be prevented by deep watering before the soil dries out.
Blackspot Usually occurs in midsummer (July or August in the UK) and spreads rapidly if not controlled. The spores only germinate if the leaves stay wet for at least seven hours when the weather is warm. Therefore, if you are watering, do so at a time when the leaves can dry out relatively quickly - usually in the morning. There is a great deal of variability in resistance between varieties, although most have the potential to develop blackspot.
Rust This appears as bright orange and later black pustules on the undersides of the leaves and occasionally stems. It occurs in cool weather, early or more likely late in the season. It is more difficult to eradicate but spraying will at least hold it back.
Downy Mildew Is not so common as the other three and is rather hard to detect. One sure sign is when the leaves begin to drop prematurely. Downy mildew tends to occur when you have low night temperatures and high humidity in the day. Because of that, you tend to get it earlier and later in the season. It is a disease that is found only on certain varieties.
In sect pests are usually less of a problem than disease. They are easily controlled by spraying with a proprietary insecticide. Alternatively encourage as many beneficial insects into your garden as possible as they can be most effective.

The Lifespan of a Rose
Finally, there is the question of 'How long does a rose actually live?' This is rather like asking 'How long is a piece of string?' However there is no doubt that there comes a point when any rose will begin to deteriorate. There is often a gradual decline. Before this becomes too steep, it is probably best to dig the rose up and replace it. On the whole, it is repeat-flowering roses that tend to die earliest; they are under greater strain to produce flowers throughout the summer. The once-flowering Old Roses can go on living for a very long time indeed; this is perhaps the reason why they have remained with us to the present day.

Glossary

Anther The part of the flower which produces pollen; the upper section of the stamen.

Arching shrub A shrub in which the long main branches bend down towards the soil, usually in a graceful manner.

Balled, balling The clinging together of petals due to damp, so that the bloom fails to open.

Bare-root roses Roses bought without soil, not in a container.

Basal shoot The strong main shoot that arises from the base of the rose.

Bicolour A rose bloom with two distinct shades of colour.

Boss The bunch of stamens at the centre of a flower.

Bract A modified leaf at the base of a flower stalk.

Break New growth from a branch.

Budding The usual method for the propagation of roses by the grafting of a leaf bud on to the neck of a root stock.

Bud-shaped flower I have coined this term to describe rose blooms that are in the form of a Hybrid Tea, i.e. flowers that are of high-centred bud formation and mainly beautiful in the bud (as opposed to those of Old Rose formation).

Bud Union The point where the rose stems join the root stock.

Bush I use this word to describe a closely pruned bedding rose, as for example a Hybrid Tea.

Bushy shrub A rose of dense, rounded growth.

Button Eye A button-like fold of petals in the centre of a rose bloom.

Calyx The green protective cover over the flower bud which opens into five sepals.

Cane A long rose stem, from the base of the plant, particularly as in a Rambling Rose.

Chromosomes Chains of linked genes contained in the cells of plants and animals.

Climbing sport See Sport; the climbing form of this phenomenon.

Corymb A flower cluster that is flat-topped, or nearly so.

Cross See Hybrid.

Cultivar Plant raised or selected in cultivation.

Denomination The intellectual nomenclature recognised world wide under the auspices of plant breeders' rights and patents.

Die back The progressive dying back of a shoot from the tip.

Diploid A plant with two sets of chromosomes.

Flore Pleno Double flower.

Flush A period of blooming.

Gene A unit of heredity controlling inherited characteristics of a plant.

Genus, genera A group or groups of plants having common characteristics, e.g. *Rosa*.

Group The name for cultivars that have similar characteristics

Heeling-in Temporary planting of roses when conditions are not suitable for permanent planting.

Height The heights given for individual varieties are only approximate. Much will depend on soil, site, season and geographic area. The breadth of a rose bush or shrub will usually be slightly less than the height.

Hips, heps Seed pods of a rose.

Hybrid A rose resulting from crossing two different species or varieties.

Leaflets The individual sections of a leaf.

Modern appearance, rose of Rose that usually has high-pointed buds and smooth foliage, similar to a Hybrid Tea Rose.

Mutation See Sport.

Old appearance, rose of Rose with bloom of cupped or rosette shape, rather than the pointed bud and informal flower of a Modern Rose; the plant usually having rough textured leaves, i.e. Gallica, Centifolia, etc.

Organic fertilizer A fertilizer made from natural materials rather than chemicals.

Patent appellation The variety denomination which is protected by Plant Breeders' Rights worldwide

Perpetual flowering A rose that continues to flower in the same year after the first flush of bloom, though not necessarily continually.

Pistil Female organ of a flower consisting of the stigma, style and ovary.

Pollen parent The male parent of a variety.

Pompon A small rounded bloom with regular short petals.

Quartered A flower in which the centre petals are folded into four.

Quilled petals Petals folded in the form of a quill.

Rambler-like I use this term to describe roses bearing large sprays of small blooms similar to those of a small-flowered Rambling Rose, particularly a Multiflora Rambler.

Recessive gene A gene that is dominated by another, rendering it ineffective unless two copies of the gene are present.

Recurrent flowering See Perpetual flowering.

Remontant See Perpetual flowering.

Repeat flowering See Perpetual flowering.

Roots, roses on their own Not budded on to a stock; grown from cuttings.

Root stock The host plant on to which a cultivated variety is budded.

Rugose Leaves with a wrinkled surface.

Scion A shoot or bud used for grafting on to a root stock.

Seedling A rose grown from seed. In the context of this book, the offspring of a variety.

Sepal One of the five green divisions of the calyx.

Shrub A rose that is normally pruned lightly and allowed to grow in a more natural form, as opposed to a bush which is pruned close to the ground.

Species A wild rose.

Sport A change in the genetic make up of the plant, as for example when a pink rose suddenly produces a white flower.

Spreading shrub A shrub on which the branches tend to extend outwards rather than vertically.

Stamen The male organ of a flower, consisting of the filament and anther, which produces pollen.

Stigma The end of the pistil or female flower organ.

Stock See Root-stock

Style The stem of the pistil which joins the stigma to the ovary.

Sucker A shoot growing from the root stock instead of from the budded variety.

Tetraploid A plant with four sets of chromosomes.

Trade designation See Denomination.

Triploid A plant with three sets of chromosomes.

Upright shrub A rose in which the growth tends to be vertical.

Variety Strictly speaking, a naturally occurring variation of a species. The popular meaning, so far as roses are concerned, is a distinct type of cultivated rose.

✕ Indicates a hybrid

Bibliography

American Rose Society's *Annuals*, from 1917.

Austin, David *The English Roses*, Conran Octopus, 2005.

Bean, W.J., *Trees and Shrubs Hardy in the British Isles*, Murray, 8th edn. revised.

Bois, Eric and Trechslin, Anne-Marie, *Roses*, 1962.

Bunyard, A.E., *Old Garden Roses*, Collingridge, 1936.

Dobson, B.R., *Combined Rose List. Hard to Find Roses and Where to Find Them*, Beverly R. Dobson, Irvington, New York 10533, 1985.

Edwards, G., *Wild and Old Garden Roses*, David & Charles, Newton Abbot, 1975; Hafner, New York, 1975.

Ellwanger, H.B., *The Rose*, Dodd-Mead, New York, 1822; 1914.

Fisher, John, *The Companion to Roses*, Viking, 1986

Fletcher, H.L.V., *The Rose Anthology*, Newnes, 1963.

Foster-Melliar, Rev. A., *The Book of the Rose*, Macmillan, 1894; 1910.

Gault S.M. and Synge P.M., *The Dictionary of Roses in Colour*, Michael Joseph and Ebury Press, 1970.

Gore, C.F., *The Book of Roses or The Rose Fancier's Manual*, 1838; Heyden, 1978.

Griffiths, Trevor, *The Book of Old Roses*, Michael Joseph, 1984.

Griffiths, Trevor, *The Book of Classic Old Roses*, Michael Joseph, 1986.

Harkness, Jack, *Roses*, Dent, 1978.

Hillier Manual of Trees and Shrubs, The, 3rd rev edn, David & Charles 2007.

Hole, S. Reynolds, *A Book about Roses*, William Blackwood, 1896.

Hollis, L., *Roses*, Collingridge, 1969; 2nd edn. with new illustrations, 1974.

Jekyll, G. and Mawley, E., *Roses for English Gardens*, Country Life, 1902; reprinted by Antique Collectors' Club, Woodbridge, 1982.

Keays, F.L., *Old Roses*, Macmillan, New York, 1935; facsimile edn. Heyden, Philadelphia and London, 1978.

Kordes, Wilhelm, *Roses*, Studio Vista, 1964.

Krussman, G., *Roses*, English edn, Batsford, 1982.

Lawrence, Mary, *A Collection of Roses* from Nature, 1799.

Le Grice, E.B., *Rose Growing Complete*, Faber & Faber, 1965.

Lord, Tony, *Designing with Roses*, Frances Lincoln, 1999.

McFarland, J.H., *Modern Roses*, 8th edn, McFarland Co., USA, 1980.

McFarland, J.H., *Roses of the World in Colour*, Cassell, 1936.

Mansfield, T.C., *Roses in Colour and Cultivation*, Collins, 1947.

Nottle, T., *Growing Old Fashioned Roses in Australia and New Zealand*, Kangaroo Press, 1983.

Olson, Jerry and John Whitman, *Growing Roses in Cold Climates*, Contemporary Books, 1998.

Paul, William, *The Rose Garden*, 10th edn, Simpkin, Marshall, Hamilton, Kent & Co., 1903.

Pemberton, Rev. J.H., *Roses, Their History, Development and Cultivation*, Longmans Green 1908; rev. edn. 1920.

Phillips, Roger and Rix, Martyn, *The Ultimate Guide to Roses*, Macmillan, 2004.

Quest-Ritson, Charles and Brigid, *The Royal Horticultural Society Encyclopaedia of Roses*, Dorling Kindersely, 2005.

Redouté, P.J., *Les Roses*, 1817–24, reprinted by Taschen, 2001.

RHS Plantfinder 2007–2008, Dorling Kindersely, 2007.

Ridge, A., *For the Love of a Rose*, Faber & Faber, 1965.

Rivers, T., *The Rose Amateur's Guide*, Longmans Green, 1837.

Ross, D., *Shrub Roses in Australia*, Deane Ross, 1981.

Royal National Rose Society's *Annuals*, from 1911.

Shepherd, R., *History of the Rose*, Macmillan, New York, 1966.

Steen, N., *The Charm of Old Roses*, Herbert Jenkins, 1966.

Thomas, G.S., *The Old Shrub Roses*, Phoenix House, 1955.

Thomas, G.S., *Shrub Roses of Today*, Phoenix House, 1962.

Thomas, G.S., *Climbing Roses Old and New*, Phoenix House, 1965.

Thompson, Richard, *Old Roses for Modern Gardens*, Van Nostrand, New York, 1959.

Warner, C., *Climbing Roses*, Tiptree Books.

Willmott, Ellen, *The Genus Rosa*, Murray, issued in parts 1910–14.

Young, Norman, *The Complete Rosarian*, Hodder & Stoughton, 1971.

Index

Figures in italics indicate an illustration